GED**X**celerator PREP — Reading

STUDENT BOOK

PA**X**EN

PA**X**EN

Melbourne, Florida
www.paxen.com

Acknowledgements

For each of the selections and images listed below, grateful acknowledgement is made for permission to excerpt and/or reprint original or copyrighted material, as follows:

Text

2 Used with the permission of *The Atlantic*, © 2008 **5** From American Rhetoric, www.americanrhetoric.com. "Inaugural Address" by John F. Kennedy ©1961; From American Rhetoric, www.americanrhetoric.com. "Checkers" by Richard M. Nixon © 1952 **6** Excerpts reprinted with permission by *Car and Driver* **8** Reprinted by permission of Don Congdon Associates, Inc. Copyright © 1968 by Edward Abbey, renewed 1996 by Clarke Abbey **9** From SAVAGE INEQUALITIES by Jonathan Kozol, copyright ©1991 by Jonathan Kozol. Used by permission of Crown Publishers, a division of Random House, Inc. **10** Used with permission of The Associated Press Copyright © 2007 **11** From the New York Times, July 24 © 2008 The New York Times All rights reserved. Used by permission and protected by the Copyright Laws of the United States. The printing, copying, redistribution, or retransmission of the Material withought express written permission is prohibited. **12** Used with the permission of the University of New Mexico. "The Way to Rainy Mountain" by N. Scott Momaday, originally published in *The Way to Rainy Mountain* © 1969 **14** From the New York Times, October 7 © 1960 The New York Times All rights reserved. Used by permission and protected by the Copyright Laws of the United States. The printing, copying, redistribution, or retransmission of the Material withought express written permission is prohibited. **15** From Newsweek, December 11 © 2007 Newsweek, Inc. All rights reserved. Used by permission and protected by the Copyright Laws of the United States. The printing, copying, redistribution, or retransmission of the Material withought express written permission is prohibited. **17** Reprinted by permission of International Creative Management, Inc. Copyright © 1990 by Barbara Ehrenreich **18** From the New York Times, June 29 © 2008 The New York Times All rights reserved. Used by permission and protected by the Copyright Laws of the United States. The printing, copying, redistribution, or retransmission of the Material withought express written permission is prohibited. **19** Used with the permission of Susan Estrich. Originally published in The New York Times, June 12 © 1994 **20** From the New York Times, August 7 © 2008 The New York Times All rights reserved. Used by permission and protected by the Copyright Laws of the United States. The printing, copying, redistribution, or retransmission of the Material withought express written permission is prohibited. **21** From the New York Times, June 10 © 2008 The New York Times All rights reserved. Used by permission and protected by the Copyright Laws of the United States. The printing, copying, redistribution, or retransmission of the Material withought express written permission is prohibited. **22** From American Rhetoric, www.americanrhetoric.com. "Democratic National Convention Keynote Address" by Barbara Jordan © 1976 **23** From American Rhetoric, www.americanrhetoric.com. "A Time for Choosing" Ronald Reagan © 1976 **24** Used with the permission of Malcolm Gladwell. "Annals of Public Policy: Troublemakers." Originally published in *The New Yorker* ©2006 **26** From the New York Times, August 19 © 2008 The New York Times All rights reserved. Used by permission and protected by the Copyright Laws of the United States. The printing, copying, redistribution, or retransmission of the Material without express written permission is prohibited. **35** From THE STORIES OF JOHN CHEEVER by John Cheever, copyright © 1978 by John Cheever. Used by permission of Alfred A. Knopf, a division of Random House, Inc. **36** Copyright © 1961 Tillie Olsen from TELL ME A RIDDLE, reprinted by permission of the Frances Goldin Literary Agency. **37** Used with the permission of James A. McPherson. Originally published in *Elbow Room* © 1972 **40** Excerpt from "He" in FLOWERING JUDAS AND OTHER STORIES, copyright 1930 and renewed 1958 by Katherine Anne Porter, reprinted by permission of Houghton Mifflin Harcourt Publishing Company. **41** Reprinted with the permission of Scribner, a Division of Simon & Schuster, Inc., from ROMAN FEVER AND OTHER STORIES by Edith Wharton. Copyright © 1934 by Liberty Magazine. Copyright renewed © 1962 by William R. Tyler. All rights reserved. **42** Used with the permission of Pam Durban. Originally published in *The Southern Review* © 1996 **43** "Criers and Kibitzers, Kibitzers and Criers" by Stanley Elkin. Copyright © 1965 by Stanley Elkin. Reprinted by permission of Georges Borchardt, Inc., on behalf of the Estate of Stanley Elkin. **44** Used with the permission of Joyce Carol Oates. Originally published in *Epoch* © 1966 **45** Excerpt from "the Circling Hand" from ANNIE JOHN by Jamaica Kincaid. Copyright © 1985 by Jamaica Kincaid. Reprinted by permission of Farrar, Straus and Giroux, LLC. **46** "The Rocking Horse Winner," by D. H. Lawrence, © 1928. Published in *The Woman who Rode Away and Other Stories*, by Cambridge University Press, © 1995. Reproduced by permission of the Estate of Frieda Lawrence Ravagli and Pollinger Limited. **47** Reprinted by permission of International Creative Management, Inc. Copyright © 1988 by Bobbie Ann Mason. **48** From "Physics" by Tama Janowitz, originally published in *Wonderful Town: New York Stories from the New Yorker* © 1985. Used with the permission of Dunow, Carlson & Lerner Literary Agency. **49** Reprinted by permission of International Creative Management, Inc. Copyright © 1940 by Walter Van Tilburg Clark

ISBN-13: 978-1-934350-22-5
ISBN-10: 1-934350-22-2

2 3 4 5 6 7 8 9 10 GEDXSE4 16 15 14 13 12 11 10

Printed in the U.S.A.

Images

Table of Contents

About the GED Tests

Simply by turning to this page, you've made a decision that will change your life for the better. Each year, thousands of people just like you decide to pursue the General Education Development (GED) certificate. Like you, they left school for one reason or another. And now, just like them, you've decided to continue your education by studying for and taking the GED Tests.

However, the GED Tests are no easy task. The tests—five in all, spread across the subject areas of Language Arts/Reading, Language Arts/Writing, Mathematics, Science, and Social Studies—cover slightly more than seven hours. Preparation time takes considerably longer. The payoff, however, is significant: more and better career options, higher earnings, and the sense of achievement that comes with a GED certificate. Employers and colleges and universities accept the GED certificate as they would a high school diploma. On average, GED recipients earn more than $4,000 per year than do employees without a GED certificate.

The GED Tests have been constructed by the American Council on Education (ACE) to mirror a high-school curriculum. Although you will not need to know all of the information typically taught in high school, you will need to answer a variety of questions in specific subject areas. In Language Arts/Writing, you will need to write an essay on a topic of general knowledge.

In all cases, you will need to effectively read and follow directions, correctly interpret questions, and critically examine answer options. The table below details the five subject areas, the amount of questions within each of them, and the time that you will have to answer them. Since different states have different requirements for the amount of tests you may take in a single day, you will need to check with your local adult education center for requirements in your state or territory.

The original GED Tests were released in 1942 and since have been revised a total of three times. In each case, revisions to the tests have occurred as a result of educational findings or workplace needs. All told, more than 17 million people have received a GED certificate since the tests' inception.

SUBJECT AREA BREAKDOWN	CONTENT AREAS	ITEMS	TIME LIMIT
Language Arts/Reading	Literary texts—75% Nonfiction texts—25%	40 questions	65 minutes
Language Arts/Writing (Editing)	Organization—15% Sentence Structure—30% Usage—30% Mechanics—25%	50 questions	75 minutes
Language Arts/Writing (Essay)	Essay	Essay	45 minutes
Mathematics	Number Sense/Operations—20% to 30% Data Measurement/Analysis—20% to 30% Algebra—20% to 30% Geometry—20% to 30%	Part I: 25 questions (with calculator) Part II: 25 questions (without calculator)	90 minutes
Science	Life Science—45% Earth/Space Science—20% Physical Science—35%	50 questions	80 minutes
Social Studies	Geography—15% U.S. History—25% World History—15% U.S. Government/Civics—25% Economics—20%	50 questions	70 minutes

Three of the subject-area tests—Language Arts/Reading, Science, and Social Studies—will require you to answer questions by interpreting passages. The Science and Social Studies tests also require you to interpret tables, charts, graphs, diagrams, timelines, political cartoons, and other visuals. In Language Arts/Reading, you also will need to answer questions based on workplace and consumer texts. The Mathematics Test will require you to use basic computation, analysis, and reasoning skills to solve a variety of word problems, many of them involving graphics. On all of the tests, questions will be multiple-choice with five answer options. An example follows:

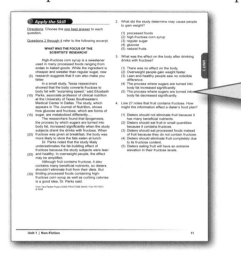

On the Mathematics test, you will have additional ways in which to register your responses to multiple-choice questions.

As the table on p. vi indicates, the Language Arts/ Writing Test contains two parts, one for editing, the other for essay. In the editing portion of Language Arts/ Writing, you will be asked to identify and correct common errors in various passages and texts while also deciding on the most effective organization of a text. In the essay portion, you will write an essay that provides an explanation or an opinion on a single topic of general knowledge.

So now that you understand the task at hand—and the benefits of a GED certificate— you must prepare for the GED Tests. In the pages that follow, you will find a recipe of sorts that, if followed, will help guide you toward successful completion of your GED certificate. So turn the page. The next chapter of your life begins right now.

About *GED Prep Xcelerator*

Along with choosing to pursue your GED certificate, you've made another smart decision by selecting *GED Prep Xcelerator* as your main study and preparation tool. Simply by purchasing *GED Prep Xcelerator*, you've joined an elite club with thousands of members, all with a common goal—earning their GED certificates. In this case, membership most definitely has its privileges.

For more than 65 years, the GED Tests have offered a second chance to people who need it most. To date, 17 million Americans like you have studied for and earned GED certificates and, in so doing, jump-started their lives and careers. Benefits abound for GED holders: Recent studies have shown that people with GED certificates earn more money, enjoy better health, and exhibit greater interest in and understanding of the world around them than those without.

In addition, more than 60 percent of GED recipients plan to further their educations, which will provide them with more and better career options. As if to underscore the point, U.S. Department of Labor projections show that 90 percent of the fastest-growing jobs through 2014 will require postsecondary education.

Your pathway to the future—a brighter future—begins now, on this page, with *GED Prep Xcelerator*, an intense, accelerated approach to GED preparation. Unlike other programs, which take months to teach the GED Tests through a content-based approach, *Xcelerator* gets to the heart of the GED Tests—and quickly—by emphasizing *concepts*. That's because at their core, the majority of the GED Tests are reading-comprehension exams. You must be able to read and interpret excerpts, passages, and various visuals—tables, charts, graphs, timelines, and so on—and then answer questions based upon them.

Xcelerator shows you the way. By emphasizing key reading and thinking concepts, *Xcelerator* equips learners like you with the skills and strategies you'll need to correctly interpret and answer questions on the GED Tests. Two-page micro-lessons in each student book provide focused and efficient instruction, while call-out boxes, sample exercises, and test-taking and other thinking strategies aid in understanding complex concepts. For those who require additional support, we offer the *Xcelerator* workbooks, which provide twice the support and practice exercises as the student books.

Unlike other GED materials, which were designed for the classroom, *Xcelerator* materials were designed *from* the classroom, using proven educational theory and cutting-edge classroom philosophy. The result: More than 90 percent of people who study with *Xcelerator* earn their GED certificates. For learners who have long had the deck stacked against them, the odds are finally in their favor. And yours.

GED BY THE NUMBERS

17 million
Number of GED recipients since the inception of GED tests

1.23 million
Amount of students who fail to graduate from high school each year

700,000
Number of GED test-takers each year

451,759
Total number of students who passed the GED Tests in 2007

$4,000
Average additional earnings per year for GED recipients

About *GED Prep Xcelerator Reading*

For those who think the GED Language Arts/Reading Test is a breeze, think again. The GED Language Arts/Reading Test is a rigorous exam that will assess your ability to understand and interpret subject-specific passages. You will have a total of 65 minutes in which to answer 40 multiple-choice questions organized across four main content areas: Non-fiction (25% of all questions) and Fiction, Poetry, and Drama (which combine for 75% of all questions). Material in *GED Prep Xcelerator Reading* has been organized with these percentages in mind.

GED Prep Xcelerator Reading helps unlock the learning and deconstruct the different elements of the test by helping learners like you to build and develop key reading and thinking skills. A combination of targeted strategies, informational call-outs and sample questions, assorted tips and hints (including Test-Taking Tips, Using Logic, and Making Assumptions), and ample assessment help to clearly focus study efforts in needed areas, all with an eye toward the end goal: Success on the GED Tests.

As on the GED Social Studies and Science tests, the Language Arts/Reading Test will *not* test you on any knowledge outside of that presented in the text. The GED Language Arts/Reading Test uses the thinking skills of *comprehension*, *application*, *analysis*, and *synthesis*. Certain questions on the GED Language Arts/Reading Test ask you to take information from the text and apply it to a different situation. *GED Prep Xcelerator Reading* provides a number of questions of this type for practice.

The **Learn the Skill** section defines and provides additional information about the skill to be studied.

Callouts provide strategies and information that you may use to understand and interpret various passages or graphics.

Numbers in parentheses let you know the number of lines in the excerpts.

Making Assumptions guides you to making smart, rational assumptions that will help you answer multiple-choice questions.

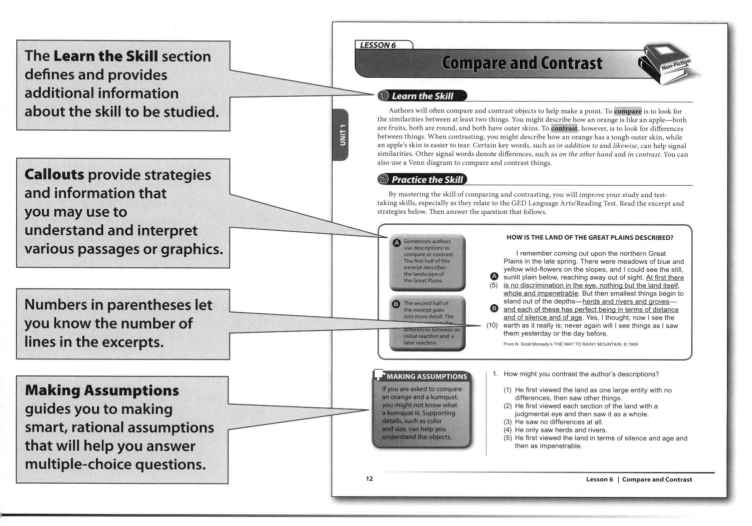

LESSON 6

Compare and Contrast

1 Learn the Skill

Authors will often compare and contrast objects to help make a point. To **compare** is to look for the similarities between at least two things. You might describe how an orange is like an apple—both are fruits, both are round, and both have outer skins. To **contrast**, however, is to look for differences between things. When contrasting, you might describe how an orange has a tough outer skin, while an apple's skin is easier to tear. Certain key words, such as *in addition to* and *likewise*, can help signal similarities. Other signal words denote differences, such as *on the other hand* and *in contrast*. You can also use a Venn diagram to compare and contrast things.

2 Practice the Skill

By mastering the skill of comparing and contrasting, you will improve your study and test-taking skills, especially as they relate to the GED Language Arts/Reading Test. Read the excerpt and strategies below. Then answer the question that follows.

A Sometimes authors use descriptions to compare or contrast. The first half of this excerpt describes the landscape of the Great Plains.

B The second half of the excerpt goes into more detail. The author contrasts the differences between an initial reaction and a later reaction.

HOW IS THE LAND OF THE GREAT PLAINS DESCRIBED?

I remember coming out upon the northern Great Plains in the late spring. There were meadows of blue and yellow wild-flowers on the slopes, and I could see the still, **(A)** sunlit plain below, reaching away out of sight. <u>At first there (5) is no discrimination in the eye, nothing but the land itself, whole and impenetrable.</u> But then smallest things begin to stand out of the depths—<u>herds and rivers and groves— **(B)** and each of these has perfect being in terms of distance and of silence and of age.</u> Yes, I thought, now I see the (10) earth as it really is; never again will I see things as I saw them yesterday or the day before.

From N. Scott Momady's THE WAY TO RAINY MOUNTAIN, © 1969

MAKING ASSUMPTIONS

If you are asked to compare an orange and a kumquat, you might not know what a kumquat is. Supporting details, such as color and size, can help you understand the objects.

1. How might you contrast the author's descriptions?

(1) He first viewed the land as one large entity with no differences, then saw other things.
(2) He first viewed each section of the land with a judgmental eye and then saw it as a whole.
(3) He saw no differences at all.
(4) He only saw herds and rivers.
(5) He first viewed the land in terms of silence and age and then as impenetrable.

12   Lesson 6 | Compare and Contrast

Test-Taking Tips

The GED Tests include 240 questions across the five subject-area exams of Language Arts/Reading, Language Arts/Writing, Mathematics, Science, and Social Studies. In each of the GED Tests, you will need to apply some amount of subject-area knowledge. However, because all of the questions are multiple-choice items largely based on text or visuals (such as tables, charts, or graphs), the emphasis in *GED Prep Xcelerator* is on helping learners like you to build and develop core reading and thinking skills. As part of the overall strategy, various test-taking tips are included below and throughout the book to help you to improve your performance on the GED Tests. For example:

◆ *Always thoroughly read the directions so that you know exactly what to do.* In Mathematics, for example, one part of the test allows for the use of a calculator. The other part does not. If you are unsure of what to do, ask the test provider if the directions can be explained.

◆ *Read each question carefully so that you fully understand what it is asking.* Some questions, for example, may present extra information that is unnecessary to correctly answer them. Other questions may note emphasis through capitalized and boldfaced words (Which of the following is **NOT** an example of photosynthesis?).

◆ *Manage your time with each question.* Because the GED Tests are timed exams, you'll want to spend enough time with each question, but not *too* much time. For example, on the GED Science Test, you will have 80 minutes in which to answer 50 multiple-choice questions. That works out to a little more than 90 seconds per item. You can save time by first reading each question and its answer options before reading the passage or examining the graphic. Once you understand what the question is asking, review the passage or visual for the appropriate information.

◆ *Note any unfamiliar words in questions.* First attempt to re-read a question by omitting any unfamiliar word(s). Next, try to substitute another word in its place.

◆ *Answer all questions, regardless of whether you know the answer or are guessing at it.* There is no benefit in leaving questions unanswered on the GED Tests. Keep in mind the time that you have for each test and manage it accordingly. For time purposes, you may decide to initially skip questions. However, note them with a light mark beside the question and try to return to them before the end of the test.

◆ *Narrow answer options by re-reading each question and the accompanying text or graphic.* Although all five answers are possible, keep in mind that only one of them is correct. You may be able to eliminate one or two answers immediately; others may take more time and involve the use of either logic or assumptions. In some cases, you may need to make your best guess between two options. If so, keep in mind that test-makers often avoid answer patterns; that is, if you know the previous answer is (2) and are unsure of the answer to the next question but have narrowed it to options (2) and (4), you may want to choose (4).

◆ *Read all answer choices.* Even though the first or second answer choice may appear to be correct, be sure to thoroughly read all five answer choices. Then go with your instinct when answering questions. For example, if your first instinct is to mark (1) in response to a question, it's best to stick with that answer unless you know that answer is incorrect. Usually, the first answer you choose is the correct one.

◆ *Correctly complete your answer sheet by marking one numbered space on the answer sheet beside the number to which it corresponds.* Mark only one answer for each item; multiple answers will be scored as incorrect. If time permits, double-check your answer sheet after completing the test to ensure that you have made as many marks—no more, no less—as there are questions.

Study Skills

You've already made two very smart decisions in trying to earn your GED certificate and in purchasing *GED Prep Xcelerator* to help you do so. The following are additional strategies to help you optimize success on the GED Tests.

3 weeks out ...

- Set a study schedule for the GED Tests. Choose times in which you are most alert, and places, such as a library, that provide the best study environment.

- Thoroughly review all material in *GED Prep Xcelerator*, using the *GED Prep Xcelerator Reading Workbook* to extend understanding of concepts in the *GED Prep Xcelerator Reading Student Book*.

- Make sure that you have the necessary tools for the job: sharpened pencils, pens, paper, and, for Mathematics, the Casio-FX 260 Solar calculator.

- Keep notebooks for each of the subject areas that you are studying. Folders with pockets are useful for storing loose papers.

- When taking notes, restate thoughts or ideas in your own words rather than copying them directly from a book. You can phrase these notes as complete sentences, as questions (with answers), or as fragments, provided you understand them.

- Take the pretests, noting any troublesome subject areas. Focus your remaining study around those subject areas.

1 week out ...

- Prepare the items you will need for the GED Tests: admission ticket (if necessary), acceptable form of identification, some sharpened No. 2 pencils (with erasers), a watch, eyeglasses (if necessary), a sweater or jacket, and a high-protein snack to eat during breaks.

- Map out the course to the test center, and visit it a day or two before your scheduled exam. If you drive, find a place to park at the center.

- Get a good night's sleep the night before the GED Tests. Studies have shown that learners with sufficient rest perform better in testing situations.

The day of ...

- Eat a hearty breakfast high in protein. As with the rest of your body, your brain needs ample energy to perform well.

- Arrive 30 minutes early to the testing center. This will allow sufficient time in the event of a change to a different testing classroom.

- Pack a sizeable lunch, especially if you plan to be at the testing center most of the day.

- Focus and relax. You've come this far, spending weeks preparing and studying for the GED Tests. It's your time to shine.

Before You Begin: Using Logic and Making Assumptions

At more than seven hours in length, the GED Tests are to testing what marathons are to running. Just like marathons, though, you may train for success on the GED Tests. As you know, the exams test your ability to interpret and answer questions about various passages and visual elements. Your ability to answer such questions involves the development and use of core reading and thinking skills. Chief among these are the skills of reasoning, logic, and assumptions.

Reasoning involves the ability to explain and describe ideas. **Logic** is the science of correct reasoning. Together, reasoning and logic guide our ability to make and understand assumptions. An **assumption** is a belief that we know to be true and which we use to understand the world around us.

You use logic and make assumptions every day, sometimes without even knowing that you're doing so. For example, you might go to bed one night knowing that your car outside is dry; you might awaken the next morning to discover that your car is wet. In that example, it would be *reasonable* for you to *assume* that your car is wet because it rained overnight. Even though you did not see it rain, it is the most *logical* explanation for the change in the car's appearance.

When thinking logically about items on the GED Tests, you identify the consequences, or answers, from text or visuals. Next, you determine whether the text or visuals logically and correctly support the consequences. If so, they are considered valid. If not, they are considered invalid. For example, read the following text and determine whether each passage is valid or invalid:

Passage A

The GED Tests assess a person's reading comprehension skills. Ellen enjoys reading. Therefore, Ellen will do well on the GED Tests.

Passage B

The GED Tests cover material in five different subject areas. Aaron has geared his studies toward the tests, and he has done well on practice tests. Therefore, Aaron may do well on the GED Tests.

Each of the above situations has a consequence: *Ellen will* or *Aaron may do well* on the GED Tests. By using reasoning and logic, you can make an assumption about which consequence is valid. In the example above, it is *unreasonable* to assume that Ellen will do well on the GED Tests simply because she likes to read. However, it *is* reasonable to assume that Aaron may do well on the GED Tests because he studied for and did well on the practice tests in each of the five subject areas.

Use the same basic principles of reasoning, logic, and assumption to determine which answer option logically and correctly supports the question on the GED Reading Test. You may find occasions in which you have narrowed the field of possible correct answers to two, from which you must make a best, educated guess. In such cases, weigh both options and determine the one that, reasonably, makes the most sense.

You can apply these same skills when analyzing the questions on the GED Language Arts/Reading Test. Use the sample question, annotated responses, and callouts below to begin developing your logic and reasoning skills. Remember to think about the most *reasonable* and *logical* conclusions or consequences before making any *assumptions*.

For me the work week begins on Thursday, which I usually spend in patrolling the roads and walking out the trails. On Friday I inspect the campgrounds, haul firewood, and distribute toilet paper. Saturday and Sunday are my busy days as I deal with the influx of weekend visitors and campers, answering questions, pulling cars out of the sand, lowering children down off the rocks, tracking lost grandfathers and investigating picnics. My Saturday night campfire talks are brief and to the point. "Everything all right?" I say, badge and all, ambling up to what looks like a cheerful group. "Fine," they'll say; "how about a drink?" "Why not?" I say.

From Edward Abbey's INDUSTRIAL TOURISM AND NATIONAL PARKS, © 1968

Which of the following activities would the author most enjoy as a hobby?

A The red X tells you that this answer choice is incorrect. The words explain the connection to logic and reasoning.

(1) needlepoint

✗ UNREASONABLE *Nothing in the passage indicates that the speaker would enjoy an activity such as needlepoint.*

B The italicized text explains why the answer choice is not reasonable, not logical, or a bad assumption.

(2) carpentry

✗ NOT LOGICAL *Make sure you pay attention to all of the information about the excerpt. The byline tells you that the author is writing about national parks, which aim to conserve the natural beauty of the wilderness. While a person who works for the national parks may also enjoy carpentry, it is not the best answer.*

(3) hunting

✗ POOR ASSUMPTION *The same argument as to why the author would likely not enjoy carpentry applies to hunting. The author works for an organization that provides a sanctuary to wild animals, therefore it is not reasonable to assume that he would enjoy hunting animals for sport.*

(4) debate group

✗ NOT LOGICAL *While the author does seem to enjoy speaking with people, he seems friendly and non-confrontational.*

C The red checkmark tells you that this answer choice is correct. This is the most logical choice.

(5) kayaking

✔ LOGICAL *The author clearly enjoys outdoor activities, and would likely have a hobby that took him outside and among nature. Of the options provided, this is the best, most reasonable answer.*

D The highlighted text explains why this answer is the most logical choice.

① ② ③ ④ ●

Unit 1

FRAN LEBOWITZ

Fran Lebowitz studied hard to learn how to write and to obtain her GED certificate.

For Fran Lebowitz, reading was the key to good writing. Lebowitz truly began to hone her craft after she left high school without her diploma. She learned the mechanics of strong storytelling by reading the work of others. Often. As she notes,

> **Until I was about 7, I thought books were just there, like trees. When I learned that people actually wrote them, I wanted to, too.**

Lebowitz ultimately pursued and obtained her GED certificate and worked a number of odd jobs before landing a position as columnist at the magazine *Interview*. She also wrote for other magazines, such as *Mademoiselle*, before venturing into books. Her first book, a collection of essays called *Metropolitan Life*, was published in 1978. That effort was followed by *Social Studies* in 1981.

Through those works and others, Lebowitz became known for sharp-witted commentaries on human nature. Reviewers referred to her dry and sarcastic style as "urban cool." However, for more than a decade Lebowitz suffered from writer's block. During that time, she gave lectures and even guest-starred on television series such as *Law & Order*. In 1994, she returned to writing with the release of her first children's book *Mr. Chas and Lisa Sue Meet the Pandas*. For Lebowitz, the book was a labor of love. As she says,

> **To me, nothing can be more important than giving children books.**

BIO BLAST: Fran Lebowitz

- Born October 27, 1950, in Morristown, New Jersey
- Worked as a magazine columnist
- Wrote best-selling books that reflect her sharp wit and sarcastic style
- Wrote a children's book called *Mr. Chas and Lisa Sue Meet the Pandas*

Non-Fiction

Unit 1: Non-Fiction

Whether at work, at home, or places in-between, you likely read various newspaper, magazine, and Web articles every day. Odds are that most of these articles are non-fiction pieces whose primary purpose is to inform and educate. At work, for example, you may need to read an employee manual to better understand a job-related policy. At home, you may need to read instructions to successfully use your new Mp3 player.

Similarly, non-fiction pieces play a vital role in the GED Language Arts/Reading Test. As with other areas of the GED Tests, questions about non-fiction works will test your ability to read and interpret passages through the use of various reading skills. In Unit 1, the introduction of skills such as summarizing, categorizing, sequencing, and generalizing will help you prepare for the GED Language Arts/Reading Test.

Table of Contents

Main Idea and Details

① Learn the Skill

The **main idea** of a text is the most important point of the passage. The main idea is usually found in the topic sentence of a paragraph, and may be in the beginning, middle, or end of a passage. **Supporting details** provide additional information about the main idea. These details can include facts, statistics, examples, or descriptions.

② Practice the Skill

By mastering the skill of identifying the main idea and supporting details, you will improve your study and test-taking skills, especially as they relate to the GED Language Arts/Reading Test. Read the excerpt and strategies below. Then answer the question that follows.

Ⓐ By reading the underlined text, you know that the main idea of this passage is the effectiveness of teachers trained by Teach for America.

Ⓑ The second sentence provides supporting details, giving the reader additional information about the main idea.

WHY DID RESEARCHERS PERFORM THE STUDY?

However, the first study to examine Teach for America at the secondary-school level, recently released by the
Ⓐ Urban Institute, <u>finds that its teachers are in fact more effective than those with traditional training</u>—at all levels
(5) of experience. <u>The study measured performance on state exams and found that students of Teach for America</u>
Ⓑ <u>instructors did significantly better in all subject areas tested, and especially in math and science</u>. The authors found that even though the program's teachers are
(10) assigned to "the most demanding classrooms," they're able to compensate for their lack of experience with better academic preparation and motivation.

From The Atlantic's, THE KIDS ARE ALRIGHT, © 2008

💡 USING LOGIC

Questions will often indirectly ask you to find the main idea or supporting detail of a passage or paragraph. For example, you may be asked "What is the author trying to say?"

1. Which line from the text contains a detail that supports the idea that the Teach for America program trains valuable teachers?

   (1) "…Teach for America program, which recruits top college graduates."
   (2) "…have long questioned whether the program's instructors are properly prepared."
   (3) "…citing evidence that links teacher effectiveness to experience."
   (4) "…the first study to examine Teach for America at the secondary-school level."
   (5) "…finds that its teachers are in fact more effective than those with traditional training."

 **Apply the Skill**

Directions: Choose the <u>one best answer</u> to each question.

<u>Questions 2 and 3</u> refer to the following excerpt.

WHAT IS THE MAIN IDEA OF THE LETTER?

Redlands Community College

To: Redlands Community College Department Heads
From: Marissa Vega, Human Resources Director
Date: May 8
(5) **Memorandum: Guidelines for Appropriate Summer Attire**

Each employee of Redlands Community College is responsible for reporting to work in a clean, neat manner. Proper attire has a positive image on Redlands, fostering public confidence and a professional environment.

As we approach the summer season, I would like to review the "summer business casual" dress
(10) code. As a reminder, the Personnel Dress Code in the Redlands Employee Handbook states:

Department heads shall determine appropriate attire for the employees under their supervision. Employees are expected to wear clothing suitable to their job and work site.

Department heads should use their discretion in determining how the employees in their departments may adapt to summer weather with more casual clothing. However, the following are
(15) clearly not acceptable at Redlands Community College:

• Tight-fitting or transparent clothing
• Shirts with potentially offensive words or logos
• Clothing that shows the midriff, such as low jeans or short shirts

If an employee's clothing fails to meet department standards, the supervisor should clarify why the
(20) item is inappropriate and instruct the individual to not wear it again.

---

2. Why is the human resources director distributing this memorandum?

(1) She has learned of inappropriate summer clothing.
(2) She hopes to suggest alternative summer attire.
(3) She intends to discipline department heads.
(4) She needs to introduce a new dress code policy.
(5) She wants to clarify the summer dress code policy.

3. Based on this memo, when would it be appropriate for a manager to ask an employee to not wear an item of clothing to work in an insurance office?

(1) It is never appropriate.
(2) It is always appropriate for managers to critique employees' attire.
(3) Managers could instruct employees not to wear shirts with rude slogans.
(4) A manager should ask employees to avoid wearing pins with political statements.
(5) Employees should be advised if they wear cheaply made brands.

UNIT 1

Summarize

① Learn the Skill

When you **summarize** a text, you are restating the main points of the piece in your own words. The first step to summarizing is to locate the main ideas. A summary should include all of the main ideas, assertions, or findings, as well as other significant information the author provides. Questions that begin with *who*, *what*, *when*, *where*, *why*, and *how* can help you identify ideas that should be included.

② Practice the Skill

By mastering the skill of summarizing, you will improve your study and test-taking skills, especially as they relate to the GED Language Arts/Reading Test. Read the excerpt and strategies below. Then answer the question that follows.

(A) A summary should give the most important information. In this passage, we learn important information about the main character, Bruce Wayne.

(B) Pay close attention to the words the author uses. A summary should not include the author's point of view. This author explains one result of an event without bias.

WHY IS BATMAN'S HISTORY IMPORTANT?

The Batman franchise adds to its chronicles with its 2005 release of the prequel *Batman Begins*. **(A)** <u>The movie gives its audience a taste of its main character, Bruce Wayne, prior to his becoming the caped crusader of Gotham. As Batman he is trying to avenge the death</u> (5) <u>of his parents</u>. Before Batman puts on his bat suit and drives off in the batmobile equipped with fancy gadgets, the audience learns about Bruce Wayne the boy and young man. **(B)** <u>As a boy, Bruce falls into a well full of</u> (10) <u>bats. This event scares him and comes to represent his biggest fears</u>. Later as a rich Ivy Leaguer, he decides to leave Princeton to take a journey to the Himalayas. There he is trained in martial arts in order to gain the strength that will eventually turn him into Batman.

✓ TEST-TAKING TIPS

This review is a summary of a movie. The author identified the important parts of the movie and described them briefly, without judgment. Think about how you might summarize your favorite movie.

1. What does the summary tell us about Bruce Wayne?

Bruce Wayne

(1) only goes to an Ivy League school because he is rich
(2) would rather contemplate his past than focus on his future
(3) is very content as a student at Princeton
(4) would rather seek his education outside the walls of Princeton
(5) enjoys his formal education

Questions 4 and 5 refer to the following excerpt.

Directions: Choose the <u>one best answer</u> to each question.

Questions 2 and 3 refer to the following excerpt.

HOW DOES THE SPEAKER FEEL ABOUT HIS COUNTRY?

In the long history of the world, only a few generations have been granted the role of defending freedom in its hour of maximum danger. I do not shrink from this

(5) responsibility —I welcome it. I do not believe that any of us would exchange places with any other people or any other generation. The energy, the faith, the devotion which we bring to this endeavor will light our country and all

(10) who serve it. And the glow from that fire can truly light the world.

And so, my fellow Americans, ask not what your country can do for you; ask what you can do for your country.

(15) My fellow citizens of the world, ask not what America will do for you, but what together we can do for the freedom of man.

From John F. Kennedy's INAUGURAL ADDRESS, © 1961

2. What responsibility does the speaker welcome in lines 3 through 5?

The speaker welcomes the responsibility to

(1) govern a country with energy and faith
(2) help bring light to the rest of the world
(3) support American's rights
(4) speak to other citizens of the world
(5) defend freedom in its hour of danger

3. What is the speaker's main point in lines 11 through 13?

(1) Americans should be willing to work for their country.
(2) Americans should allow their country to work for them.
(3) Americans should not question their government.
(4) Americans should rely on themselves, not on their government.
(5) Americans should understand the importance of their country.

WHAT DOES THE SPEAKER FEEL IS HIS BEST OPTION?

I come before you tonight as a candidate for the Vice Presidency and as a man whose honesty and integrity has been questioned.

Now, the usual political thing to do when
(5) charges are made against you is to either ignore them or to deny them without giving details. I believe we've had enough of that in the United States, particularly with the present Administration in Washington, D.C.

(10) To me the office of the Vice Presidency of the United States is a great office, and I feel that the people have got to have confidence in the integrity of the men who run for that office and who might obtain it.

From Richard M. Nixon's CHECKERS, © 1952

4. In lines 1 through 3, the speaker says his honesty and integrity have been questioned. According to him, what is the political thing to do when charges are made?

According to the speaker, the political thing to do when charges are made against a person is to

(1) question those charges
(2) refute those charges
(3) explain the merit of the charges
(4) ignore or deny those charges
(5) provide details of the charges

5. Which of the following best summarizes the passage?

(1) The speaker says that his honor has been upheld.
(2) The speaker wants people to forget about voting.
(3) The speaker believes that people should have faith in him.
(4) The speaker believes he has been justly accused of wrongdoing.
(5) The speaker does not believe he has the confidence of the people.

UNIT 1

Categorize

Non-Fiction

① Learn the Skill

Categorizing can help you organize information into groups. You can sort many elements, such as people, events, places, and even texts, into groups based on their similarities or differences. Categories are typically broad, such as *Regions of the United States* or *Animals of Asia.*

② Practice the Skill

By mastering the skill of categorizing, you will improve your study and test-taking skills, especially as they relate to the GED Language Arts/Reading Test. Read the excerpt and strategies below. Then answer the question that follows.

A The first line in this excerpt names a car company and refers to "car buyers." From this information, you know that you will be categorizing cars.

B The word "sedan" at the beginning of sentence and the term "mid-size segment" at the end let you know to categorize kinds of car models.

WHY DID MAZDA REDESIGN THE MAZDA 6?

A Executives from Mazda are betting that car buyers looking for a new sedan who might ordinarily lean towards the Toyota Camry or Honda Accord will give serious consideration to the new 2009 Mazda 6, which has been
(5) designed specifically to match up with those rivals in the **B** mid-size segment.
      "This is the most important new vehicle Mazda has launched in a decade," said Mazda North America CEO Jim O'Sullivan.
(10) The first new Mazda 6s rolled off the assembly line at the Auto Alliance Plant in Flat Rock, Michigan, this week and O'Sullivan couldn't be happier. "We think sales of 100,000 units are within our grasp," says O'Sullivan, acknowledging that the old version of the Mazda 6
(15) had dropped off the shopping lists prepared by a lot of consumers.

From Joseph Szczesny's 2009 MAZDA 6 A CRUCIAL LAUNCH, © 2008

USING LOGIC

While categorizing, you may come across an object that you think should be put into a category, but you might not know what category. Clues from the sentence in which the object appears can indicate the correct category for that object.

1. Into which size group is the author categorizing the 2009 Mazda 6?

   (1) SUV
   (2) compact
   (3) luxury
   (4) subcompact
   (5) mid-size

Directions: Choose the <u>one best answer</u> to each question.

<u>Questions 2 and 3</u> refer to the following excerpt.

WHAT OPTIONS ARE PROVIDED FOR MR. JACKSON?

Eric Jackson
Jackson Homes
330 Plum Street
Sioux City, IO 51101

(5) Dear Mr. Eric Jackson,

Thank you for your interest in a line of credit with Greenville Bank. We currently have a variety of options available for our business customers. These options are listed below.

Option 1: $250,000 credit line with 6.9% APR for members who have an annual income of $75,000 or more.

(10)   Option 2: $250,000 credit line with 7.9% APR for members who have an annual income between $50,000 and $75,000.

Option 3: $250,000 credit line with 8.9% APR for members who have an annual income under $50,000.

These options do not include conditions that may lower your monthly payments, such as down
(15) payments, collateral, and co-signees. If you would like to consider options that do include such conditions, please schedule an appointment with a Greenville Bank Credit Specialist at your earliest convenience.

Greenville Bank has a long-standing history of quality customer care and excellent service. We appreciate your interest in our banking services, and look forward to hearing from you.

(20) Thank you,

George Sanders
Credit Specialist
Greenville Bank

2. Mr. Jackson currently has an annual salary of $63,000. Based on this information, into which category might he fall?

(1) approved for option 1
(2) approved for option 2
(3) approved for option 3
(4) not approved
(5) approved with special conditions

3. Based on this letter, how might a person with a down payment be categorized?

(1) He or she may be ineligible for a credit line.
(2) He or she may get a higher APR.
(3) He or she would not need a credit line.
(4) He or she may get a lower monthly payment.
(5) He or she would need to choose option 1.

Sequence

Non-Fiction

① Learn the Skill

A passage's **sequence** is the order in which events occur. Often when reading non-fiction writing, identifying the sequence of events in chronological order is important to help you understand the relationships between events. For example, if you understand the sequence of a newspaper story, you will be better able to analyze how one event in the story may have led to another. If an author does not use dates, he or she may use signal words. These signal words, such as *first*, *next*, *then*, and *finally,* will help you determine the sequence.

② Practice the Skill

By mastering the skill of identifying sequence, you will improve your study and test-taking skills, especially as they relate to the GED Language Arts/Reading Test. Read the excerpt and strategies below. Then answer the question that follows.

A When you read a story, it may help to create a time line sequence. This piece organizes events by days of the week.

B Progression is the way in which a story moves forward. This story progresses by the passing of days.

WHAT IS THE AUTHOR'S ROUTINE?

For me the work week begins on Thursday, which I usually spend in patrolling the roads and walking out the trails. On Friday I inspect the campgrounds, haul firewood, and distribute toilet paper. Saturday and Sunday are my
(5) busy days as I deal with the influx of weekend visitors and campers, answering questions, pulling cars out of the sand, lowering children down off the rocks, tracking lost grandfathers and investigating picnics. My Saturday night campfire talks are brief and to the point. "Everything all
(10) right?" I say, badge and all, ambling up to what looks like a cheerful group. "Fine," they'll say; "how about a drink?" "Why not?" I say.

From Edward Abbey's INDUSTRIAL TOURISM AND NATIONAL PARKS, © 1968

✓ TEST-TAKING TIPS

Instructional and business writings are often the easiest pieces of writing in which to determine the sequence. Instructions will tell you the order in which steps must be done. Business writing will often explain how a business transaction occurred.

1. Which line from the excerpt best describes what the author does first in his work week?

    (1) "...I inspect the campgrounds."
    (2) "...I deal with the influx of weekend visitors and campers."
    (3) "...I usually spend in patrolling the roads and walking out the trails."
    (4) "...haul firewood, and distribute toilet paper."
    (5) "My Saturday night campfire talks are brief..."

Directions: Choose the <u>one best answer</u> to each question.

<u>Questions 2 through 5</u> refer to the following excerpt.

HOW DOES THE AUTHOR FEEL ABOUT THE SCHOOL SYSTEM?

I had begun to teach in 1964 in Boston in a segregated school so crowded and so poor that it could not provide my fourth grade children with a classroom. We shared an
(5) auditorium with another fourth grade and the choir and a group that was rehearsing, starting in October, for a Christmas play that, somehow, never was produced. In the spring I was shifted to another fourth grade that had
(10) a string of substitutes all year. The 35 children in the class hadn't had a permanent teacher since they entered kindergarten. That year, I was their thirteenth teacher.

The results were seen in the first tests I
(15) gave. In April, most were reading at the second grade level. Their math ability was at the first grade level.

In an effort to resuscitate their interest, I began to read them poetry I liked. They were
(20) drawn especially to poems of Robert Frost and Langston Hughes. One of the most embittered children in the class began to cry when she first heard the words of Langston Hughes....

The next day, I was fired. There was, it
(25) turned out, a list of "fourth grade poems" that teachers were obliged to follow but which, like most first-year teachers, I had never seen.

From Jonathan Kozol's SAVAGE INEQUALITIES: CHILDREN IN AMERICA'S SCHOOLS, © 1991

2. What was the author doing in the spring of 1965?

    (1) sharing an auditorium for a classroom
    (2) reading poetry to a new fourth grade class
    (3) working with students for a Christmas play that never was produced
    (4) being fired for teaching poetry
    (5) working at a suburban school in Boston

3. Which action led to the author being fired from his job?

    (1) teaching a text that was not approved
    (2) encouraging student interest in the lessons
    (3) never producing a Christmas play
    (4) teaching students to read on a second grade level
    (5) sharing a classroom with another teacher

4. Which meaning does the author intend when he writes that "the results were seen in the first tests I gave" (lines 14–15)?

    (1) The students were very well prepared for their tests.
    (2) The constant changing of teachers had not prepared students for the tests.
    (3) The students' test results were strong.
    (4) The students could read and do math.
    (5) The tests were designed for kindergarten students.

5. Based on the excerpt, which of the following most likely happened next?

    (1) The author went to work for the city government.
    (2) Poems by Robert Frost and Langston Hughes were approved to be taught to fourth graders.
    (3) The author began to teach at another school.
    (4) The Christmas play was produced.
    (5) The author began to teach first graders.

Cause and Effect

Non-Fiction

① Learn the Skill

A traffic accident blocks the road you travel to get to work. You choose to take another route. This is an example of cause and effect in action. A **cause** is an action that makes another event happen. Many times, a cause will be directly stated in a text, although sometimes it will be implied. An **effect** is something that happens as the result of a cause. In the example above, the traffic accident is the cause, and having to find a new route is the effect. In a non-fiction text, signal words such as *accordingly*, *because*, *consequently*, *as a result*, *therefore*, *so*, *then*, and *to this end* can help you determine a cause and its effect.

② Practice the Skill

By mastering the skill of identifying causes and their effects, you will improve your study and test-taking skills, especially as they relate to the GED Language Arts/Reading Test. Read the excerpt and strategies below. Then answer the question that follows.

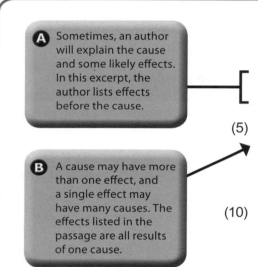

A Sometimes, an author will explain the cause and some likely effects. In this excerpt, the author lists effects before the cause.

B A cause may have more than one effect, and a single effect may have many causes. The effects listed in the passage are all results of one cause.

WHAT IS THE MAIN IDEA OF THE PASSAGE?

As the world gets hotter by degrees, millions of poor people will <u>suffer from hunger, thirst, floods and disease unless drastic action is taken</u>, scientists and diplomats warned Friday in their bleakest report ever on <u>global</u>
(5) <u>warming</u>.

All regions of the world will change, with the risk that nearly a third of the Earth's species will vanish if global temperatures rise just 3.6 degrees above the average temperature in the 1980s-90s, the new climate report
(10) says. Areas that now have too little rain will become drier.

From The Associated Press, PANEL OFFERS WARNING ON GLOBAL WARMING, © 2007

USING LOGIC

Signal words can appear to guide your reading for cause and effect, but sometimes they do not. In some instances, you can find the cause or the effect by connecting key ideas or details to one another.

1. Based on this excerpt, what will cause millions of people to suffer from hunger?

   (1) cooling weather
   (2) floods
   (3) disease
   (4) global warming
   (5) science

Directions: Choose the <u>one best answer</u> to each question.

<u>Questions 2 through 4</u> refer to the following excerpt.

WHAT WAS THE FOCUS OF THE SCIENTISTS' RESEARCH?

High-fructose corn syrup is a sweetener used in many processed foods ranging from sodas to baked goods. While the ingredient is cheaper and sweeter than regular sugar, new
(5) research suggests that it can also make you fatter.

In a small study, Texas researchers showed that the body converts fructose to body fat with "surprising speed," said Elizabeth
(10) Parks, associate professor of clinical nutrition at the University of Texas Southwestern Medical Center in Dallas. The study, which appears in The Journal of Nutrition, shows how glucose and fructose, which are forms of
(15) sugar, are metabolized differently....

The researchers found that lipogenesis, the process by which sugars are turned into body fat, increased significantly when the study subjects drank the drinks with fructose. When
(20) fructose was given at breakfast, the body was more likely to store the fats eaten at lunch.

Dr. Parks noted that the study likely underestimates the fat-building effect of fructose because the study subjects were lean
(25) and healthy. In overweight people, the effect may be amplified.

Although fruit contains fructose, it also contains many beneficial nutrients, so dieters shouldn't eliminate fruit from their diets. But
(30) limiting processed foods containing high-fructose corn syrup as well as curbing calories is a good idea, Dr. Parks said.

From Tara Parker-Pope's DOES FRUCTOSE MAKE YOU FATTER?, © 2008

2. What did the study determine may cause people to gain weight?

(1) processed foods
(2) high-fructose corn syrup
(3) regular sugar
(4) glucose
(5) natural fruits

3. What was the effect on the body after drinking drinks with fructose?

(1) There was no effect on the body.
(2) Overweight people gain weight faster.
(3) Lean and healthy people saw no noticeable difference.
(4) The process where sugars are turned into body fat increased significantly.
(5) The process where sugars are turned into body fat decreased significantly.

4. Line 27 notes that fruit contains fructose. How might this information effect a dieter's food plan?

(1) Dieters should not eliminate fruit because it has many beneficial nutrients.
(2) Dieters should eat fruit in small quantities because it contains fructose.
(3) Dieters should eat processed foods instead of fruit because they do not contain fructose.
(4) Dieters should eliminate fruit completely due to its fructose content.
(5) Dieters eating fruit will have an extreme elevation in their fructose levels.

Compare and Contrast

Non-Fiction

① Learn the Skill

Authors will often compare and contrast objects to help make a point. To **compare** is to look for the similarities between at least two things. You might describe how an orange is like an apple—both are fruits, both are round, and both have outer skins. To **contrast**, however, is to look for differences between things. When contrasting, you might describe how an orange has a tough outer skin, while an apple's skin is easier to tear. Certain key words, such as *in addition to* and *likewise*, can help signal similarities. Other signal words denote differences, such as *on the other hand* and *in contrast*. You can also use a Venn diagram to compare and contrast things.

② Practice the Skill

By mastering the skill of comparing and contrasting, you will improve your study and test-taking skills, especially as they relate to the GED Language Arts/Reading Test. Read the excerpt and strategies below. Then answer the question that follows.

Ⓐ Sometimes authors use descriptions to compare or contrast. The first half of this excerpt describes the landscape of the Great Plains.

Ⓑ The second half of the excerpt goes into more detail. The author contrasts the differences between an initial reaction and a later reaction.

HOW IS THE LAND OF THE GREAT PLAINS DESCRIBED?

I remember coming out upon the northern Great Plains in the late spring. There were meadows of blue and yellow wild-flowers on the slopes, and I could see the still, sunlit plain below, reaching away out of sight. **Ⓐ** <u>At first there</u>
(5) <u>is no discrimination in the eye, nothing but the land itself, whole and impenetrable</u>. But then smallest things begin to stand out of the depths—<u>herds and rivers and groves—</u>
Ⓑ <u>and each of these has perfect being in terms of distance and of silence and of age</u>. Yes, I thought, now I see the
(10) earth as it really is; never again will I see things as I saw them yesterday or the day before.

From N. Scott Momady's THE WAY TO RAINY MOUNTAIN, © 1969

🧩 MAKING ASSUMPTIONS

If you are asked to compare an orange and a kumquat, you might not know what a kumquat is. Supporting details, such as color and size, can help you understand the objects.

1. How might you contrast the author's descriptions?

   (1) He first viewed the land as one large entity with no differences, then saw other things.
   (2) He first viewed each section of the land with a judgmental eye and then saw it as a whole.
   (3) He saw no differences at all.
   (4) He only saw herds and rivers.
   (5) He first viewed the land in terms of silence and age and then as impenetrable.

Directions: Choose the <u>one best answer</u> to each question.

<u>Questions 2 and 3</u> refer to the following excerpt.

WHAT NEW POLICY IS OUTLINED IN THE MEMORANDUM?

Memorandum
To: WaveLength Team Members and Contractors
From: WaveLength Security Department
Date: November 9
(5) Subject: New Badge Policy

Currently, WaveLength employees and contractors may gain access into the buildings on the WaveLength campus by showing a number of types of photo identification. To avoid miscommunications and other security issues, the following badge policy will be in effect beginning Monday, November 15. This policy is mandatory, and **no exceptions** will be made.

(10)   **New WaveLength Facility Badge Policy**

- All employees and contractors must wear their WaveLength badges AT ALL TIMES while in the facility. Previous policy required that badges or IDs be shown only at point of entry.
- Badges must be clearly VISIBLE at all times. Clothing should not obstruct a clear view of the badge. Employees customarily have worn badges on shirt pockets, where they could be obscured
(15)   by jackets or sweaters. Please note the change.
- Employees and contractors MUST swipe their badges at the door, even if the door is already open. Previously, employees entering open doors with groups of people have held up cards to show them to security guards.
- Employees and contractors who do not have badges upon arrival at work MUST enter the building through
(20)   the main doors to obtain a temporary badge. Security guards will no longer be allowed to gain authorization from department heads or other supervisor.
- If you observe ANYONE in the building not wearing a badge, escort that person IMMEDIATELY to the front desk.

2. Based on the information in this memo, how does the new badge policy compare with the previous policy?

   (1) The new policy applies only to contractors, not to employees.
   (2) The new policy is more strict than the old policy was.
   (3) The old policy allowed access only to people with badges.
   (4) The old policy required all employees to enter by the front desk.
   (5) Both policies require supervisors to give employees' access to the building.

3. What type of business might consider making changes suggested in this memo?

   (1) a sports arena
   (2) a farmer's market
   (3) a shopping center
   (4) a grocery store
   (5) a child care facility

Fact and Opinion

Non-Fiction

1 Learn the Skill

When reading a passage of non-fiction text, it is important to determine what is fact and what is opinion. Some texts are based on facts, such as a piece of scientific writing that includes figures like "two-thirds of the planet is covered in water." A **fact** is a piece of information that can be proven true or untrue. Other texts are based on opinions, such as an editorial in a newspaper. An **opinion** is a person's view or judgment and cannot be proven true or untrue.

2 Practice the Skill

By mastering the skill of determining facts from opinions, you will improve your study and test-taking skills, especially as they relate to the GED Language Arts/Reading Test. Read the excerpt and strategies below. Then answer the question that follows.

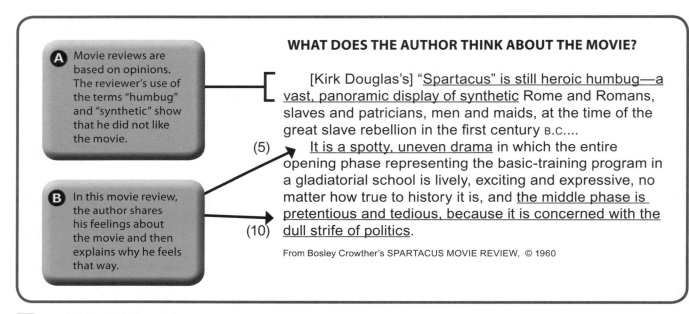

A Movie reviews are based on opinions. The reviewer's use of the terms "humbug" and "synthetic" show that he did not like the movie.

B In this movie review, the author shares his feelings about the movie and then explains why he feels that way.

WHAT DOES THE AUTHOR THINK ABOUT THE MOVIE?

[Kirk Douglas's] "Spartacus" is still heroic humbug—a vast, panoramic display of synthetic Rome and Romans, slaves and patricians, men and maids, at the time of the great slave rebellion in the first century B.C....

(5) It is a spotty, uneven drama in which the entire opening phase representing the basic-training program in a gladiatorial school is lively, exciting and expressive, no matter how true to history it is, and the middle phase is pretentious and tedious, because it is concerned with the

(10) dull strife of politics.

From Bosley Crowther's SPARTACUS MOVIE REVIEW, © 1960

🧩 MAKING ASSUMPTIONS

To determine if a piece is based on fact or opinion, you might make assumptions based on the language the author uses. Look for words or phrases that sound unscientific or sensational, such as "a great book" or "a miserable experience." These phrases cannot be proven true or untrue.

1. Which line best represents an opinion from the excerpt?

   (1) "…Rome and Romans, slaves and patricians, men and maids…"
   (2) "…no matter how true to history it is…"
   (3) "…basic training program in a gladiatorial school is lively, exciting, and expressive…"
   (4) "…the entire opening phase…"
   (5) "…at the time of the great slave rebellion in the first century B.C."

UNIT 1

Directions: Choose the <u>one best answer</u> to each question.

<u>Questions 2 through 4</u> refer to the following excerpt.

WHAT ISSUE IS THE AUTHOR PRESENTING?

This is the real world of eating and nutrition in the rural United States. Forget plucking an apple from a tree, or an egg from under a chicken. "The stereotype is everyone in rural
(5) America lives on a farm, which is far from the truth," says Jim Weill, president of the nonprofit Food Research and Action Center (FRAC). New research from the University of South Carolina's Arnold School of Public Health
(10) shows just how unhealthy the country life can be. The study, which examined food-shopping options in Orangeburg County (1,106 square miles, population 91,500) found a dearth of supermarkets and grocery stores. Of the 77
(15) stores that sold food in Orangeburg County in 2004, when the study was done, 57—nearly 75 percent—were convenience stores. Grocery stores, which stock far more fruits and vegetables than convenience stores, are often
(20) too far away, says University of South Carolina epidemiologist Angela Liese, lead author of the study, which appeared in last month's Journal of the American Dietetic Association. "Oftentimes a nutritionist will just say, 'Buy
(25) more fruits and vegetables,' when, in fact, the buying part is not simple."
     Like other rural areas (and some inner-city ones), Orange County is an isolated "food desert." "You are pretty much at the mercy
(30) of what's in your neighborhood," says Adam Drewnowski, director of the center for obesity research at the University of Washington. Although only 28 percent of all the stores in Orangeburg County carried any of the fruits
(35) and vegetables—apples, cucumbers, oranges, tomatoes—that were part of the survey, Liese and her colleagues found plenty of healthy foods in the county's 20 supermarkets and grocery stores. The situation in the
(40) convenience stores was decidedly grimmer.

From Karen Springen's JUNK FOOD COUNTY, © 2007

2. Why is the author writing about this topic?

   She wants to

   (1) show the benefits of country living
   (2) demonstrate the kinds of eating habits associated with country living
   (3) discuss numerous nutrition studies
   (4) prove that people in the country shop mainly at grocery stores
   (5) show that the nutrition value of convenience store foods is poor

3. How does the author present information in this piece?

   (1) by using supporting statistics and studies
   (2) by presenting a list of pros and cons for country living
   (3) by posing her opinion about rural areas
   (4) by critically judging the studies done on food buying
   (5) by offering a solution based on the information

4. Which fact supports the idea that rural areas are considered "an isolated 'food desert'" (lines 28–29)?

   (1) people's food choices are limited to what they can grow
   (2) rural areas are isolated from people just as some inner-city areas are
   (3) people often have to travel great distances for any kind of food
   (4) people are limited to the foods and stores available in their neighborhoods
   (5) people cannot find food of any sort in their neighborhoods

Make Inferences

Non-Fiction

① Learn the Skill

Occasionally when reading non-fiction, details that are necessary to understanding the piece are only suggested, or implied. To understand what the author is saying, you must use the stated, or explicit, information as well as the implied information to **make an inference**. An inference is an idea that is supported by facts that are presented in a passage. Readers make inferences when they use suggestions, clues, or facts presented in a text to figure out what an author is saying.

② Practice the Skill

By mastering the skill of making inferences, you will improve your study and test-taking skills, especially as they relate to the GED Language Arts/Reading Test. Read the excerpt and strategies below. Then answer the question that follows.

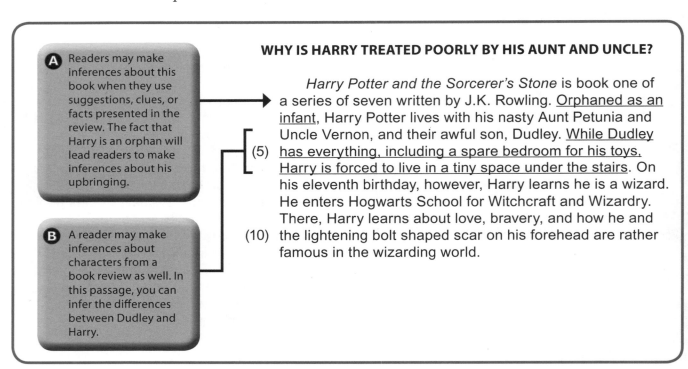

A Readers may make inferences about this book when they use suggestions, clues, or facts presented in the review. The fact that Harry is an orphan will lead readers to make inferences about his upbringing.

B A reader may make inferences about characters from a book review as well. In this passage, you can infer the differences between Dudley and Harry.

WHY IS HARRY TREATED POORLY BY HIS AUNT AND UNCLE?

Harry Potter and the Sorcerer's Stone is book one of a series of seven written by J.K. Rowling. <u>Orphaned as an infant</u>, Harry Potter lives with his nasty Aunt Petunia and Uncle Vernon, and their awful son, Dudley. <u>While Dudley</u>
(5) <u>has everything, including a spare bedroom for his toys, Harry is forced to live in a tiny space under the stairs</u>. On his eleventh birthday, however, Harry learns he is a wizard. He enters Hogwarts School for Witchcraft and Wizardry. There, Harry learns about love, bravery, and how he and
(10) the lightening bolt shaped scar on his forehead are rather famous in the wizarding world.

💡 USING LOGIC

You can logically make an inference by examining the supporting details within a text. In this review, the main idea about Harry's living situation can help you understand the author's intent.

1. What can you infer about Aunt Petunia and Uncle Vernon?

   Aunt Petunia and Uncle Vernon

   (1) don't mind raising Harry
   (2) treat Harry better than their own son
   (3) like the idea that their nephew is a wizard
   (4) do not give Harry enough love and support
   (5) give Harry and Dudley the same attention

Directions: Choose the <u>one best answer</u> to each question.

<u>Questions 2 through 4</u> refer to the following excerpt.

WHAT IS THE AUTHOR IMPLYING THROUGH HER HUMOR?

Someone has to speak for them, because they have, to a person, lost the power to speak for themselves. I am referring to that great mass of Americans who were once known

(5) as the "salt of the earth," then as "the silent majority," more recently as the "viewing public," and now, alas, as "couch potatoes." What drives them—or rather, leaves them sapped and spineless on their reclining chairs? What

(10) are they seeking—beyond such obvious goals as a tastefully colorized version of *The Maltese Falcon*?

My husband was the first in the family to "spud out," as the expression now goes. Soon

(15) everyone wanted one of those zip-up "Couch Potato Bags," to keep warm in during David Letterman. The youngest, and most thoroughly immobilized, member of the family relies on a remote that controls his TV, stereo, and

(20) VCR, and can also shut down the neighbor's pacemaker...

But we never see the neighbors anymore, nor they us. This saddens me, because Americans used to be a great and restless

(25) people, fond of the outdoors in all of its manifestations, from Disney World to miniature golf. Some experts say there are virtues in mass agoraphobia, that it strengthens the family and reduces highway deaths. But I

(30) would point out that there are still a few things that cannot be done in the den, especially by someone zipped into a body bag. These include racquetball, voting, and meeting strange people in bars.

From Barbara Ehrenreich's SPUDDING OUT, © 1990

2. Based on the information from the excerpt, what can you infer about *The Maltese Falcon* (lines 11–12)?

The Maltese Falcon

(1) is a type of bird people could see if they went outside more
(2) is a black-and-white movie
(3) is an agoraphobe
(4) is a painting that might hang in a person's living room
(5) is a kind of outdoors game people can play

3. What is the topic of this excerpt?

(1) peoples' love of television
(2) peoples' love of outdoor activities
(3) television shows
(4) peoples' hatred of spending time with family
(5) the inability to understand why people watch television

4. What inference can be made from the third paragraph?

(1) Due to too much television, people do not go out of their homes as much as in the past.
(2) Due to television, families spend more quality time together.
(3) Due to television, people stay home more and thus there are less car accidents.
(4) Due to television, strangers have topics to discuss when meeting for the first time.
(5) Due to television, people have learned about new and interesting places to visit.

Draw Conclusions

Non-Fiction

① Learn the Skill

Drawing conclusions is similar to making inferences. As you know, an inference is an educated guess based on facts or evidence. By combining several inferences together to make a judgment, you can **draw conclusions**. Determining a cause and its effect can help you draw conclusions.

② Practice the Skill

By mastering the skill of drawing conclusions, you will improve your study and test-taking skills, especially as they relate to the GED Language Arts/Reading Test. Read the excerpt and strategies below. Then answer the question that follows.

Ⓐ The first and second sentences present facts about gas prices. You can conclude that gas in Venezuela is cheaper than gas in the United States.

Ⓑ This sentence gives you a cause and effect. One conclusion you might draw is that Venezuela has lower gas taxes than the United States.

WHY DO SOME COUNTRIES PAY MORE FOR GAS?

Ⓐ Gasoline in the United States is cheap. Not as cheap as American drivers would like, of course. And not as cheap as it is in Venezuela and other major oil-producing countries, where it is
(5) heavily subsidized. Compared to prices in most other industrialized nations, however, the American national average of $4 a gallon is a bargain.

Ⓑ The chief reason for the disparity with the high-priced nations is taxation. Take away the taxes, and the
(10) remaining gas price is similar from place to place.

From Bill Marsh's SAVORING BARGAINS AT THE AMERICAN PUMP, © 2008

🔖 MAKING ASSUMPTIONS

Drawing conclusions and making inferences both rely on making assumptions or educated guesses about a topic. If the topic or the author's purpose is not clear, carefully read the text and make assumptions that can lead to inferences or conclusions.

1. What can you conclude based on this excerpt?

(1) Gasoline in the United States averages about $4 a gallon.
(2) Gasoline in the United States is less than gasoline in Venezuela.
(3) The United States has the highest prices for gasoline in the world.
(4) Gasoline in the United States is as cheap as it is in those countries where it is highly subsidized.
(5) The United States pays higher prices for gasoline than some countries, but pays significantly less per gallon than others.

Directions: Choose the <u>one best answer</u> to each question.

<u>Questions 2 through 4</u> refer to the following excerpt.

WHAT ARE THE AUTHOR'S VIEWS ABOUT SEPARATE CLASSROOMS FOR BOYS AND GIRLS?

If schools shortchange girls, why is it surprising when the tests show that they're doing less well? It isn't just the P.S.A.T.'s, where 18,000 boys generally reach the top
(5) categories and only 8,000 girls do. While the gap has narrowed, boys also outscore girls on 11 of the 14 College Board Achievement tests, and on the A.C.T. exams and on the S.A.T.'s. It is possible to jimmy selection standards
(10) to make sure girls win more scholarships, but equal results don't count for much if those results are forced. Instead of declaring equality, society should be advancing it. The challenge isn't to get more scholarships for
(15) baton twirlers but to get more baton twirlers to take up advanced mathematics.
  One place that happens is in girls' schools and women's colleges. Sometimes separate isn't equal; it's better. Changing the way
(20) teachers teach in coed schools, changing the textbooks to make sure they talk about women as well as men, educating parents about raising daughters—all of these things make sense, since most girls will be educated in
(25) coed classrooms. But we've been talking about them for a decade, and the problems of gender bias stubbornly persist. In the meantime, for many girls, single-sex education is working….
  The evidence, though scant, is promising.
(30) In Ventura, Calif., the public high school has begun offering an all-girls Algebra II course. The girls, one teacher says, think so little of their ability that the teacher spends her time not only teaching math but also building self-
(35) confidence, repeatedly telling the girls that they're smart and that they can do it.

From Susan Estrich's SEPARATE IS BETTER, © 1994

2. Based on the excerpt, which of the following conclusions might best reflect the author's viewpoint?

   (1) Math and science are as important for girls as they are for boys.
   (2) Girls may do better in math and science if they learn in all-girl classrooms.
   (3) Girls will do better in math and science if they are taught in coed classrooms.
   (4) Girls deserve to win more scholarships based on standardized tests.
   (5) Girls perform as well as or better than boys on standardized tests in math and science.

3. Which conclusion can be drawn from the third paragraph?

   (1) Separate classrooms have no impact on education.
   (2) Teachers spend too much time enhancing girls' self-esteem.
   (3) The reactions of girls taking all-girls' math and science classes are poorer.
   (4) The evidence shown from the few schools that have offered all-girls' classes is promising.
   (5) Girls have less self-confidence when entering a coed math or science class after taking an all-girls' class.

4. What evidence from the excerpt supports the conclusion that separate is better?

   (1) "...for many girls, single-sex education is working..."
   (2) "...the teacher spends her time not only teaching math but also building self-confidence..."
   (3) "...the problems of gender bias stubbornly persist."
   (4) "...equal rights don't count for much if those results are forced."
   (5) "...changing the textbooks to make sure they talk about women as well as men, educating parents about raising daughters—all of these things make sense..."

UNIT 1

Determine Point of View

Non-Fiction

① Learn the Skill

Non-fiction texts are written with different **points of view**—the perspectives and purposes with which the author writes the piece. A reader can determine an author's point of view based on clues from the text, such as details that point out what the author likes or dislikes, the vocabulary and adjectives used to describe certain situations, even the author's interests or background.

② Practice the Skill

By mastering how to determine an author's point of view, you will improve your study and test-taking skills, especially as they relate to the GED Language Arts/Reading Test. Read the excerpt and strategies below. Then answer the question that follows.

A The byline tells you that this piece comes from a newspaper editorial. This tells us that the author is basing this piece on his or her own point of view.

B Words that have positive or negative descriptions may help indicate the author's point of view.

WHAT PROBLEM IS THE AUTHOR ADDRESSING?

The need for a criminal inquiry into the Crandall Canyon mine disaster is shockingly clear now that investigators have detailed how greedy mine operators **B** concealed danger warnings and literally chiseled
(5) underground pillar supports to the breaking point. The roof of the Utah mine collapsed last summer, killing six miners and leading three would-be rescuers to their deaths.

A From New York Times' editorial GREED ABOVE, DEATH BELOW, © 2008

✓ TEST-TAKING TIPS

Some questions might ask you to consider an author's purpose in writing. The author's point of view is often related to his or her purpose for writing. For instance, an editorial piece is usually written because the author sees some sort of problem and wants to address it.

1. Which of the following best describes the author's point of view?

   (1) the dead miners should have been more careful
   (2) mine operators are not to be trusted
   (3) people should not work in mines
   (4) the practices of mine operators need to be changed
   (5) the dangers of mining in Utah are insignificant

Directions: Choose the <u>one best answer</u> to each question.

Questions 2 through 4 refer to the following excerpt.

WHY DOES THE AUTHOR THINK THAT PARKS NEED HELP?

One piece of legislation that deserves a serious push is the National Park Service Centennial Initiative. A brainchild of Dirk Kempthorne, the Interior secretary, the
(5) initiative would use the years leading up to the park system's 100th birthday in 2016 to raise $1 billion in private money and match that with $1 billion in federal money—above and beyond normal appropriations—to rejuvenate
(10) the national parks.

As recent visitors can attest, the parks need all the help they can get. Stingy budget appropriations and decades of deferred maintenance have taken a toll on everything
(15) from park roads to day-to-day operations. In his brief tenure, Mr. Kempthorne has done several good things for the parks—including killing a potentially harmful rewrite of the service's management policies that would
(20) have promoted inappropriate commercial and recreational activities at the expense of conservation. He wants now to provide a special revenue stream by using the promise of a federal match to entice private donors to help
(25) underwrite vital projects.

The idea was so appealing that the House Natural Resources Committee approved it by a voice vote. It has languished ever since,…
The solution seems ridiculously obvious.
(30) The budget office should find the offsets (an increase in park concession fees would do the trick), and the Democratic leadership should schedule a vote. We predict that the verdict would be overwhelmingly positive, and the
(35) Senate would follow suit. The parks and their millions of visitors would be the winners, and Congress could show that it can get things done—even in an election year.

From New York Times' editorial HELP THE PARKS, © 2008

2. Based on the excerpt, which of the following best describes how the author feels the legislature should proceed?

The author feels the legislature should

(1) continue focusing on the election year
(2) withhold voting on the park initiative until after the election
(3) find the money to back the National Park Service Centennial Initiative
(4) hold another committee meeting and vote again on the issue
(5) demonstrate the importance of the National Park Service by campaigning for conservation

3. Which of the following expresses the author's overall point of view?

(1) Representatives are doing all they can to help the National Park Service.
(2) The National Park Service Centennial Initiative deserves positive attention.
(3) The National Park Service needs to rewrite management policies.
(4) The National Park Service has an above average budget that should be maintained.
(5) Commercial and recreational activities should be promoted over conservation in the parks.

4. Based on the excerpt, with which of the following statements would the author most likely agree?

(1) The National Parks Service needs more support from the federal government.
(2) The federal government works quickly to help the programs it oversees.
(3) The Democratic leadership should not vote on the proposed bill.
(4) National parks should rely on visitors to get the funding for their upkeep.
(5) Conservation of national parks is not important.

UNIT 1

Style and Tone

① Learn the Skill

Authors have specific writing **styles**, made up of the ways in which they use words to communicate thoughts or ideas. A style is sometimes determined by the type of writing. For example, a non-fiction style would be very different from a fiction or poetry style. Style can also affect an author's **tone**, which shows how the author feels about the topic. Tone is revealed through the author's choice of words.

② Practice the Skill

By mastering how to identify style and tone, you will improve your study and test-taking skills, especially as they relate to the GED Language Arts/Reading Test. Read the excerpt and strategies below. Then answer the question that follows.

A This author uses repetition as a style to emphasize the points that follow the repeated words.

B The author's tone describes the Democratic Party as one to which people can turn for change.

HOW DOES THE AUTHOR FEEL ABOUT THE DEMOCRATIC PARTY?

<u>Throughout–Throughout</u> our history, when people have looked for new ways to solve their problems and to uphold the principles of this nation, many times they have turned to political parties. They have often turned

(5) to the Democratic Party. <u>What is it? What is it about the Democratic Party that makes it the instrument the people use when they search for ways to shape their future</u>? Well I believe the answer to that question lies in our concept of governing. Our concept of governing is derived from our

(10) view of people. It is a concept deeply rooted in a set of beliefs firmly etched in the national conscience of all of us.

From Barbara Jordan's 1976 DEMOCRATIC NATIONAL CONVENTION KEYNOTE ADDRESS, © 1976

USING LOGIC

When you read an excerpt, identify the emotions that the words might evoke. In doing so, you can often determine the tone of the piece: happy, pessimistic, sorrowful, etc. This will help you determine the author's message.

1. Which of the following best describes the tone of this excerpt?

   (1) depressed
   (2) encouraging
   (3) sarcastic
   (4) condescending
   (5) patronizing

Directions: Choose the <u>one best answer</u> to each question.

<u>Questions 2 through 5</u> refer to the following excerpt.

WHAT MESSAGE IS THE SPEAKER CONVEYING?

But I have an uncomfortable feeling that this prosperity isn't something on which we can base our hopes for the future. No nation in history has ever survived a tax burden that
(5) reached a third of its national income. Today, 37 cents out of every dollar earned in this country is the tax collector's share, and yet our government continues to spend 17 million dollars a day more than the government takes
(10) in. We haven't balanced our budget 28 out of the last 34 years. We've raised our debt limit three times in the last twelve months, and now our national debt is one and a half times bigger than all the combined debts of all the nations of
(15) the world. We have 15 billion dollars in gold in our treasury; we don't own an ounce. Foreign dollar claims are 27.3 billion dollars. And we've just had announced that the dollar of 1939 will now purchase 45 cents in its total value.
(20) As for the peace that we would preserve, I wonder who among us would like to approach the wife or mother whose husband or son has died in South Vietnam and ask them if they think this is a peace that should be maintained
(25) indefinitely. Do they mean peace, or do they mean we just want to be left in peace? There can be no real peace while one American is dying some place in the world for the rest of us. We're at war with the most dangerous
(30) enemy that has ever faced mankind in his long climb from the swamp to the stars, and it's been said if we lose that war, and in so doing lose this way of freedom of ours, history will record with the greatest astonishment that
(35) those who had the most to lose did the least to prevent its happening. Well I think it's time we ask ourselves if we still know the freedoms that were intended for us by the Founding Fathers.

From Ronald Reagan's A TIME FOR CHOOSING, © 1964

2. What word best describes the tone of the first paragraph?

   (1) flamboyant
   (2) matter-of-fact
   (3) sad
   (4) opinionated
   (5) tired

3. What might be the author's intention in writing the first paragraph?

   The author intends to

   (1) congratulate the government on its budget
   (2) ask people for money
   (3) explain his uncomfortable feeling
   (4) point out the budgetary problems
   (5) propose that people save money

4. Which line best indicates that the tone of the second paragraph is one of action?

   (1) "There can be no real peace while one American is dying some place in the world for the rest of us." (lines 26–29)
   (2) "I wonder who among us would like to approach the wife or mother whose husband or son has died in South Vietnam." (lines 20–23)
   (3) "Well I think it's time we ask ourselves if we still know the freedoms that were intended for us by our Founding Fathers." (lines 36–38)
   (4) "Do they mean peace, or do they mean we just want to be left in peace?" (lines 25–26)
   (5) "We're at war with the most dangerous enemy that has ever faced mankind." (lines 29–30)

5. Which of the following best describes the author's style?

   (1) informative
   (2) ambiguous
   (3) peaceful
   (4) unpatriotic
   (5) balanced

Generalize

Non-Fiction

① Learn the Skill

A **generalization** is a broad statement that applies to a group of people, places, and events. Authors use generalizations as a kind of style, or to make a point about a group. As a reader, understanding generalizations can help you determine an author's purpose in writing.

② Practice the Skill

By understanding generalizations, you will improve your study and test-taking skills, especially as they relate to the GED Language Arts/Reading Test. Read the excerpt and strategies below. Then answer the question that follows.

Ⓐ Generalizations sometimes contain words such as *all*, *everyone, few, some,* or *usually,* such as the statement about German shepherds.

Ⓑ It is important to understand a generalization that seems valid may not be so. The generalization about pit bulls is contradicted in the last sentence.

FOR WHAT REASONS ARE PIT BULLS SEEN AS DANGEROUS?

Pit bulls, descendants of the bulldogs used in the nineteenth century for bull baiting and dogfighting, have been bred for "gameness", and thus a lowered inhibition to aggression.…A pit bull is willing to fight with little or no
(5) provocation. Pit bulls seem to have a high tolerance for pain, making it possible for them to fight to the point of exhaustion. Whereas guard dogs like <u>German shepherds</u> **Ⓐ** <u>usually attempt to restrain</u> those they perceive to be threats by biting and holding, pit bulls try to inflict the maximum
(10) amount of damage on an opponent. They bite, hold, shake, and tear. They don't growl or assume an aggressive facial expression as warning. They just attack.…
Ⓑ <u>Of course, not all pit bulls are dangerous</u>. Most don't bite anyone.

From Malcolm Gladwell's ANNALS OF PUBLIC POLICY: TROUBLEMAKERS, © 2006

🧩 MAKING ASSUMPTIONS

Understanding style and tone can help you determine if generalizations are valid. A factual style will likely indicate a valid generalization, while a tone based on the author's emotions will likely indicate invalid generalizations.

1. Which generalization might be the main idea of the first paragraph?

   (1) All German shepherds attempt to restrain those they perceive as threats.
   (2) Both pit bulls and German shepherds demonstrate a great amount of aggressiveness.
   (3) All pit bulls are vicious fighters.
   (4) All pit bulls show little to no aggression.
   (5) All pit bulls show signs of signs of facial aggression.

UNIT 1

Directions: Choose the <u>one best answer</u> to each question.

<u>Questions 2 through 4</u> refer to the following excerpt.

WHAT SERVICES DOES THIS COMPANY OFFER?

Deep Shade Tree Company: We're there for the life of your trees.

A healthy tree is like a member of the family. They give your home personality, character, and—most important in this hot climate—they provide you with cool, money-saving shade.

(5) Deep Shade has been caring for trees for 25 years, working not only to increase their leafy beauty, but also lengthen the trees' lifespan. A certified arborist is on staff for consultations and diagnosis of tree diseases.

The services we offer include:
- Pruning. Limbs on the roofs of property damage siding and shingles. In addition, they allow entry to insects and rodents. Our pruning service can save you thousands of dollars in construction repairs
(10) by removing small problem areas before they become bigger ones.
- Removal of dead or dangerous trees. Our experienced staff can evaluate the trees to see if they pose a risk of falling.
- Tree maintenance. We offer deep fertilization, ball moss removal, and web-worm treatments. Our policy is to provide your trees with the nutrients they need to be healthy, not to provide chemical
(15) treatments that could be harmful to children or pets.

Let us keep you in the shade. Contact us for an estimate. http://www.deepshadetrees.com

---

2. What fact does the pamphlet disclose about Deep Shade Tree Company?

   The reader learns that the company

   (1) has been in business for 25 years
   (2) refers clients to an arborist
   (3) maintains trees with chemical applications
   (4) repairs roof damage caused by limbs
   (5) employs strict organic policies

3. How can the company's attitude about trees be best described?

   The pamphlet suggests that trees are

   (1) liable to be stricken with numerous diseases
   (2) sources of beauty and comfort
   (3) capable of causing extensive damage
   (4) dangerous when untended
   (5) expensive to maintain

4. The company suggests that limbs be removed from building roofs. Which policy does this suggestion most resemble?

   The policy most resembles

   (1) treating a cold with bed rest and fluids
   (2) visiting the emergency room with a broken bone
   (3) taking a flu vaccination each winter
   (4) using physical therapy to strengthen a strained back
   (5) using X-rays to find the location of a fracture

Unit 1 Review

The Unit Review is structured to resemble the GED Language Arts/Reading Test. Be sure to read each question and all possible answers very carefully before choosing your answer. To record your answers, fill in the numbered circle that corresponds to the answer you select for each question in the Unit Review.

Do not rest your pencil on the answer area while considering your answer. Make no stray or unnecessary marks. If you change an answer, erase your first mark completely. Mark only one answer space for each question; multiple answers will be scored as incorrect.

Sample Question
What does the excerpt tell you about the author?

(1) The author is an expert in juvenile delinquency.
(2) The author has trouble-making children.
(3) The author researched the number of minors being held in adult facilities.
(4) The author has no interest in juvenile felons.
(5) The author has no suggestion for fixing the problem.

①②●④⑤

Questions 1 through 5 refer to the following excerpt.

WHAT SOLUTION DOES THE AUTHOR SUGGEST?

The number of minors being held in adult jails and prisons in this country has dropped substantially, according to a new study based on federal data. That's welcome news.
(5) Criminologists warn that juvenile offenders who are thrown in with adult prisoners are exposed to social pressures and develop personal contacts that make it far more likely that they will become career criminals than
(10) those held in juvenile facilities.

The study, …shows that the number of minors being held in adult facilities has decreased by 38 percent since 1999. Because of reductions in juvenile crime and
(15) arrests, among other factors, the number of children held in juvenile facilities also fell.

Congress can consolidate these gains by using aid to impose a clear federal standard: To qualify for federal juvenile-justice funds,
(20) states should have to certify that people under 18 are not being jailed as adults, except in cases involving heinous crimes like rape and murder.

Unfortunately, not all of the new data is
(25) encouraging. States still seem to be holding in juvenile facilities a great many children who should instead be treated in therapeutic programs near their homes and families. Children with drug or alcohol problems
(30) should be in treatment programs, not juvenile lockups. Therapeutic programs can turn young lives around and reduce crime….

The data also show that too many children are still being confined for minor
(35) offenses like truancy, which should be dealt with through community-based programs. Putting truants into juvenile facilities makes it more likely that they will repeatedly return to custody and become permanently entangled
(40) in the system. Congress, which tried to end this practice with the Juvenile Justice and Delinquency Prevention Act of 1974, should close the loophole that allows states to continue to confining truants.
(45) Another cause for concern is the significant racial and ethnic disparities that show up in juvenile justice data. The decline in the juvenile custody rate was significantly greater for whites than for African-
(50) Americans, who account for less than 15 percent of the youth population but nearly 40 percent of those in confinement.

From the New York Times' editorial, SOME PROGRESS ON KIDS AND JAIL, © 2008

1. For what reason might the author have written this piece?

   The author

   (1) approves in the decline of juveniles held in adult prisons
   (2) believes more data needs to be collected regarding the juvenile justice system
   (3) feels that state and federal government need to play more of a role in how children are handled by the juvenile justice system
   (4) disagrees with the information provided by criminologists regarding juveniles placed in adult prisons
   (5) feels the benefits of the decline of minors in spending time in adult prisons far outweighs the concerns

   ①②③④⑤

2. According to the excerpt, what might be an effect of holding juveniles in adult prisons?

   (1) increased maturity from being held with adults
   (2) increased likelihood of a criminal career learned from adult criminals
   (3) decreased chance of maintaining a job after jail time is served
   (4) increased chance of becoming a working part of a community
   (5) decreased chance of learning from past mistakes

   ①②③④⑤

3. Based on the excerpt, what can you generalize about truancy in most states?

   (1) The number of truants in most states is low.
   (2) Too many truants are placed in juvenile facilities.
   (3) Most states have loopholes to avoid sending truants to juvenile facilities.
   (4) Truancy rates are higher in minority groups.
   (5) Truancy has very little impact on juvenile crime rates.

   ①②③④⑤

4. How does the author propose Congress might maximize the rewards of lower juvenile crime rates?

   (1) State justice departments have to prove that minors are not being held in adult prisons, unless they commit a heinous crime, in order to get federal funding.
   (2) State justice departments have to place minors in therapeutic programs to reduce crime in order to get federal funding.
   (3) State justice departments have to continue detaining minors for truancy offenses in order to get federal funding.
   (4) State justice departments have to lower their juvenile crime rates in order to get federal funding.
   (5) State justice departments have to pay attention to disparities in order to get federal funding.

   ①②③④⑤

5. In paragraph six, the author states that the "decline in the juvenile custody rate was significantly greater for whites than for African-Americans" (lines 47–50). What is the author most likely implying?

   (1) Truant minors are more likely to be in juvenile custody.
   (2) Juveniles should be treated in therapeutic programs.
   (3) The statistics of juveniles held in adult prisons are misleading.
   (4) Racial inequalities appear in juvenile justice data.
   (5) There is a lack of Congressional involvement in the juvenile justice system.

   ①②③④⑤

WHAT IS THE PURPOSE OF THIS LETTER?

The Maple Hotel
226 Maple Street
Louisville, KY 40201

Mr. Frank Thomas, CEO
(5) Thomas Building Supplies
864 Fellows Street
Cincinnati, OH 45201

Dear Mr. Thomas,

I am writing to introduce myself to you and your associates. My name is Miranda
(10) Snyder and I am the new Sales Account Manager at The Maple Hotel.

I have learned from Pat Higgins, The Maple Hotel's former Sales Account Manager
and new Director of Sales, that your company often does business in the Louisville area
and frequents our hotel on a regular basis. We thank you so much for your business. I will
now be Thomas Building Supplies' main sales correspondent from this point forward, and
(15) am looking forward to working with you and your staff for any of your upcoming business
trips, conventions, and catering events.

Your Administrative Assistant, Angela, has scheduled a block of rooms for you and
your Board of Directors for the week of September 18th. We have you booked in our newly
renovated Maple Suite. Additionally, we will have a board room available for your use each
(20) day from 8:00 am until 2:00 pm with access to wireless Internet and conference calling.
Each day our banquet staff will provide you with a mid-morning break of coffee, teas, and
pastries, as well as lunch services.

Furthermore, as part of my introduction to The Maple Hotel's preferred guests, I would
like to offer you 500 extra Maple Points that will be added to your account renewable upon
(25) your next stay with us. As you may know, Maple Points can be used toward complimentary
rooms, dining services in our restaurant, and discounts on catering services for any
events Thomas Building Supplies may hold in the future.

I look forward to meeting you in person and working with you and your staff during
your stay with us in September, as well as any upcoming events you may be planning.
(30) If I can be of assistance in any way, please do not hesitate to call; I have included my
business card for your convenience. Thank you again for your continued business.

At your service,

Miranda Snyder, Sales Account Manager

6. Why is the author writing this letter?

She is writing to

(1) apply for a job with Thomas Building Supplies
(2) arrange a face-to-face meeting with Frank Thomas
(3) introduce herself as the new sales manager at the Maple Hotel
(4) determine how many Maple Points she has earned
(5) plan a convention at the Maple Hotel

①②③④⑤

7. What is the author implying when she writes "as part of my introduction to The Maple Hotel's preferred guests" (line 23)?

(1) The author is only introducing herself to the hotel's new guests.
(2) The author is writing letters to many people.
(3) The author is planning on scheduling a face-to-face meeting.
(4) The recipient of her letter is an important client of the Maple Hotel.
(5) The recipient of her letter is receiving it as a professional courtesy.

①②③④⑤

8. Which fact does the reader learn about Mr. Thomas from the letter?

(1) Mr. Thomas has a total of 500 Maple Points.
(2) Mr. Thomas is the CEO of a building supplies company.
(3) Mr. Thomas visits Louisville weekly.
(4) Mr. Thomas always reserves a board room when he visits the Maple Hotel.
(5) Mr. Thomas always has his board meetings catered by the Maple Hotel banquet staff.

①②③④⑤

9. Which meaning is the author implying when she writes "If I can be of assistance in any way, please do not hesitate to call" (line 30)?

The author means she will

(1) make sure she is available any time Mr. Thomas calls
(2) answer all of her phone calls
(3) refer Mr. Thomas's business to another associate at the Maple Hotel
(4) only be of assistance to Mr. Thomas and his company
(5) help Mr. Thomas schedule and modify events at the Maple Hotel

①②③④⑤

10. Based on the character of the author as provided in this letter, how does she perform her job as a sales account manager?

The author performs her job

(1) harshly
(2) cautiously
(3) caringly
(4) indifferently
(5) irresponsibly

①②③④⑤

Unit 2

WALLY AMOS

Wally Amos's recipe for success included obtaining his GED certificate.

For Wally Amos, there's no business like show business. Unless, of course, it's the cookie business. Amos, the founder of the "Famous Amos" line of cookies, learned his craft innocently enough. When he was 12 years old, Amos moved from Florida to live with his aunt in New York City. She became a parent to young Wally, right down to baking chocolate-chip cookies for him.

Amos left high school before graduation and joined the U.S. Air Force. While enlisted, Amos earned his GED certificate, which made him eligible to train at a New York Secretarial school. He was hired by the William Morris Talent Agency and soon rose from mailroom clerk to become the company's first African American agent. Eventually, Amos left to form his own theatrical management agency in California. He learned to unwind on weekends by taking up a new hobby—baking chocolate-chip cookies.

In time, Amos grew tired of show business and decided instead to bake and sell cookies under his own name. He opened the Famous Amos Chocolate Chip Cookie Store on Sunset Boulevard in Hollywood. Today, Famous Amos cookies are sold in many grocery stores across the nation.

Through his success, Amos has brought attention to the cause of literacy. For more than 20 years, Amos served as the national spokesperson for Literacy Volunteers of America. In 2005, he and his wife, Christine, created the Chip & Cookie Read-Aloud Foundation, an organization that promotes childhood literacy. Over time, Amos became a renowned author and motivational speaker whose books and lectures convey his positive attitude. As he notes,

❝ Everyone who has achieved greatness or fulfillment in life started out with a dream. ❞

BIO BLAST: Wally Amos

- Earned his GED certificate while serving in the Air Force
- Opened his own theatrical management agency in California
- Started the Famous Amos Chocolate Chip Cookie store in 1975
- Received various honors for business and literacy efforts

Fiction

Unit 2: Fiction

Fiction is one of the more popular forms of writing. Each year, millions of people read novels, short stories, and even comic books by authors who use their imaginations to create tales of adventure, romance, and mystery. Similarly, fiction pieces appear on the GED Language Arts/Reading Test.

The selections that follow are similar to those you will see on the GED Language Arts/Reading Test. On the exam, fiction is divided between prose before 1920, prose between 1920 and 1960, and prose after 1960. In Unit 2, the further use of skills such as identifying a cause and its effect, comparing and contrasting, and understanding point of view, as well as the introduction of ideas such as theme, setting, and tone, will help you prepare for the GED Language Arts/Reading Test.

Table of Contents

Context Clues

① Learn the Skill

Context clues can help you figure out the meaning of a word or a passage of text. Context means the clues, details, or restatements that surround an unknown word. Understanding how to use context clues to determine a word's meaning will help you grasp the overall idea of an excerpt.

② Practice the Skill

By mastering the skill of understanding context clues, you will improve your study and test-taking skills, especially as they relate to the GED Language Arts/Reading Test. Read the excerpt and strategies below. Then answer the question that follows.

A The second sentence provides context clues for the word *monotonous* by describing the way in which Simon Wheeler tells his story. Apparently, Wheeler never smiles, frowns, or changes his voice while telling a story.

B The words "without ever smiling" in the paragraph emphasize that the speaker tells his story without emotion or emphasis.

WHAT PROBLEM DOES THE NARRATOR HAVE WITH SIMON WHEELER?

...Simon Wheeler backed me into a corner and blockaded me there with his chair, and then sat me down and reeled off the <u>monotonous narrative</u> which follows this paragraph. He <u>never smiled, he never frowned, he never</u>
(5) <u>changed his voice from the gentle-flowing key to which he tuned the initial sentence, he never betrayed the slightest suspicion of enthusiasm</u>; but all through the interminable narrative there ran a vein of impressive earnestness and sincerity, which showed me plainly that, so far from his
(10) imagining there was any thing ridiculous or funny about his story, he regarded it as a really important matter, and admired its two heroes as men of transcendent genius in finesse. To me the spectacle of a man drifting serenely along through such a <u>queer yarn without ever smiling</u>, was
(15) exquisitely absurd.

From Mark Twain's THE CELEBRATED JUMPING FROG OF CALAVERAS COUNTY, © 1867

☑ TEST-TAKING TIPS

Context clues may come from synonyms. Check for other words in the sentence or surrounding sentences that make comparisons with an unfamiliar word.

1. The narrator says that Simon Wheeler tells a "monotonous narrative." Which statement best describes a monotonous voice?

   (1) It is loud.
   (2) It is expressive.
   (3) It has a tone that stays the same.
   (4) It has a high pitch.
   (5) It is difficult to understand.

③ *Apply the Skill*

Directions: Choose the <u>one best answer</u> to each question.

Questions 2 and 3 refer to the following excerpt.

WHY IS THE NARRATOR GETTING ON A TRAIN?

      I held a florin tightly in my hand as I strode down Buckingham Street towards the station. The sight of the streets thronged with buyers and glaring with gas recalled to me
(5) the purpose of my journey. I took my seat in a third-class carriage of a deserted train. After an intolerable delay the train moved out of the station slowly. It crept onward among ruinous houses and over the twinkling river.
(10) At Westland Row Station a crowd of people pressed to the carriage doors; but the porters moved them back, saying that it was a special train for the bazaar. I remained alone in the bare carriage. In a few minutes the train drew
(15) up beside an improvised wooden platform. I passed out on to the road and saw by the lighted dial of a clock that it was ten minutes to ten. In front of me was a large building which displayed the magical name.
(20)   I could not find any sixpenny entrance and, fearing that the bazaar would be closed, I passed in quickly through a turnstile, handing a shilling to a weary-looking man. I found myself in a big hall girdled at half its height by
(25) a gallery. Nearly all the stalls were closed and the greater part of the hall was in darkness. I recognized a silence like that which pervades a church after a service. I walked into the center of the bazaar timidly. A few people
(30) were gathered about the stalls which were still open. Before a curtain, over which the words *Café Chantant* were written in colored lamps, two men were counting money on a salver. I listened to the fall of the coins.

From James Joyce's ARABY, © 1914

2. The narrator rides in the carriage of a "deserted train" (line 6). Which of the following probably could be found in a "deserted" room?

   (1) a large party of people
   (2) a political meeting
   (3) no men, women, or children
   (4) a church service
   (5) crowds attending a bazaar

3. The narrator of the story "passed quickly through a turnstile, handing a shilling to a weary looking man." What is a shilling?

   (1) a kind of entrance
   (2) another word for a turnstile
   (3) something at a bazaar
   (4) a type of money
   (5) a church service

Question 4 refers to the following excerpt.

WHAT IS THE NARRATOR DESCRIBING?

      The hamlet of Barry's Ford is situated in a sort of high valley among the mountains. Below it the hills lie in moveless curves like a petrified ocean; above it they rise in green-
(5) cresting waves which never break. It is *Barry's* Ford because at one time the Barry family was the most important in the place; and *Ford* because just at the beginning of the hamlet the little turbulent Barry River is fordable. There is,
(10) however, now a rude bridge across the river.

From Mary E. Wilkins Freeman's OLD WOMAN MAGOUN, © 1891

4. Based on the information in the excerpt, what is a ford?

A ford is

   (1) a place to cross a river
   (2) a type of bridge
   (3) a small village
   (4) a high valley
   (5) an important family

Cause and Effect

① Learn the Skill

As you learned in Unit 1, authors often use **cause and effect** to create the events of their stories. A **cause** is an element, such as an action, that makes something happen. An **effect** is what happens as a result of that cause. What one person does in one part of the story can affect another person in another part of the story. A cause can have more than one effect, and an effect may have more than one cause.

Effects can be both positive and negative. The outcome of stories often depends on whether causes lead to effects that are planned or unplanned.

② Practice the Skill

By mastering the skill of identifying cause and effect, you will improve your study and test-taking skills, especially as they relate to the GED Language Arts/Reading Test. Read the excerpt and strategies below. Then answer the question that follows.

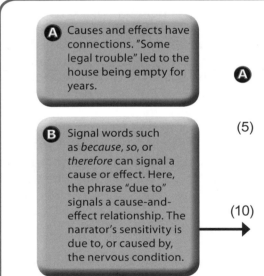

A Causes and effects have connections. "Some legal trouble" led to the house being empty for years.

B Signal words such as *because*, *so*, or *therefore* can signal a cause or effect. Here, the phrase "due to" signals a cause-and-effect relationship. The narrator's sensitivity is due to, or caused by, the nervous condition.

HOW DOES THE NARRATOR FEEL ABOUT THE HOUSE?

A So I will let it alone and talk about the house.... <u>There was some legal trouble</u>, I believe, something about the heirs and co-heirs; anyhow, the place has been empty for years.

(5) That spoils my ghostliness, I am afraid, but I don't care—there is something strange about the house—I can feel it.

I even said so to John one moonlight evening, but he said what I felt was a draught, and shut the window.

(10) I get unreasonable angry with John sometimes. I'm sure I never used to be so sensitive. <u>I think it is due to</u> this nervous condition.

From Charlotte Perkins Gilman's THE YELLOW WALLPAPER, © 1892

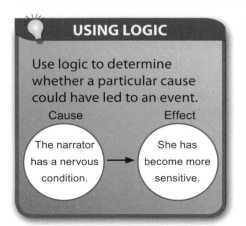

USING LOGIC

Use logic to determine whether a particular cause could have led to an event.

Cause → Effect

The narrator has a nervous condition. → She has become more sensitive.

1. What causes John to shut the window?

   (1) The narrator says there is a draft.
   (2) The narrator says the house is strange.
   (3) The narrator is cold.
   (4) John has a nervous condition.
   (5) John does not want to see the moonlight.

UNIT 2

③ Apply the Skill

Directions: Choose the <u>one best answer</u> to each question.

<u>Questions 2 through 5</u> refer to the following excerpt.

WHY DOES THE OTHER PASSENGER BEGIN TALKING TO FRANCIS?

To begin at the beginning, the airplane from Minneapolis in which Francis Weed was traveling East ran into heavy weather....Then mist began to form outside the windows, and
(5) they flew into a white cloud of such density that it reflected the exhaust fire. The color of the cloud darkened to gray, and the plane began to rock. Francis had been in heavy weather before, but he had never been shaken up so
(10) much. The man in the seat beside him pulled a flask out of his pocket and took a drink. Francis smiled at his neighbor, but the man looked away; he wasn't sharing his painkiller with anyone....Then the lights flickered
(15) and went out. "You know what I've always wanted to do?" the man beside Francis said suddenly. "I've always wanted to buy a farm in New Hampshire and raise beef cattle." The stewardess announced that they were going
(20) to make an emergency landing....[T]here was a loud shrieking high in the air, like automobile brakes, and the plane hit flat on its belly in a cornfield and shook them so violently that an old man up forward howled, "Me kidneys! Me
(25) kidneys!"

From John Cheever's THE COUNTRY HUSBAND, © 1955

2. What happens to the airplane traveling from Minneapolis?

(1) Because of delays, it arrives late.
(2) It is forced to land in another city.
(3) Bad weather causes an emergency landing.
(4) An inexperienced pilot puts it in danger.
(5) Rain and wind break a wing from the plane.

3. The passage states that "the man in the seat beside him pulled a flask out of his pocket and took a drink" (lines 10–11). Why does the man react this way?

The man probably reacts this way because he is

(1) thinking of buying a farm
(2) concerned that he will be late
(3) frightened by the storm
(4) thirsty
(5) in pain

4. Which of the following is most likely the other man's "painkiller" (line 13)?

(1) a prescription medication
(2) the heavy weather
(3) the rocking of the plane
(4) beef cattle
(5) the drink in the flask

5. What happens as the plane lands?

(1) People calmly leave their seats and exit the plane.
(2) People are killed as the plane turns over on the ground.
(3) The plane crashes and is destroyed in the cornfield.
(4) A rough landing shakes up passengers severely.
(5) The stewardess is injured as she aids the passengers.

UNIT 2

Compare and Contrast

1 Learn the Skill

Authors use **comparisons** and **contrasts** to describe parts of their stories, such as people, places, or conflicts. When authors make comparisons, they show the similarities between two or more things. When they show contrast, they emphasize the differences. Comparing and contrasting can help you sort out and analyze information. You can group details, events, or people by their similarities and differences.

2 Practice the Skill

By mastering the skills of comparing and contrasting, you will improve your study and test-taking skills, especially as they relate to the GED Language Arts/Reading Test. Read the excerpt and strategies below. Then answer the question that follows.

A Here, the author contrasts two sisters, Susan and Emily. The author describes Susan, and then says that Emily is not the same at all.

B The narrator continues to emphasize the differences between Susan and Emily, explaining that Susan is outgoing and amuses her audiences while Emily is quiet.

HOW ARE THE NARRATOR'S CHILDREN DESCRIBED?

Oh there are conflicts between the others too, each one human, needing, demanding, hurting, taking—but only between Emily and Susan, no, Emily toward Susan that corroding resentment. It seems so obvious on the surface,
(5) yet it is not obvious. Susan, the second child, <u>Susan,</u>
A <u>golden-and curly-haired and chubby, quick and articulate and assured, everything in appearance and manner Emily was not;</u> Susan, not able to resist Emily's precious things, losing or sometimes clumsily breaking them; <u>Susan telling</u>
(10) <u>jokes and riddles to company for applause while Emily sat</u>
B <u>silent</u> (to say to me later: that was my riddle, Mother, I told it to Susan)….

From Tillie Olsen's I STAND HERE IRONING, © 1961

✓ TEST-TAKING TIPS

A Venn diagram is a useful tool for organizing comparison and contrast. A comparison of Emily and Susan might look like this:

Emily   Susan

both

1. How would you compare Emily's personality traits with those of Susan's?

   (1) Emily is more outgoing than Susan.
   (2) Susan finds more riddles than Emily does.
   (3) Emily is the quick-witted sister.
   (4) Susan is the weaker sister.
   (5) Emily speaks less confidently in public than Susan.

Directions: Choose the <u>one best answer</u> to each question.

<u>Questions 2 through 5</u> refer to the following excerpt.

WHAT INFLUENCES THE NARRATOR'S MUSICAL TASTE?

No one will believe that I like country music. Even my wife scoffs when told such a possibility exists. "Go on!" Gloria tells me. "I can see blues, bebop, maybe even a little
(5) buckdancing. But not bluegrass." Gloria says, "Hillbilly stuff is not just music. It's like the New York Stock Exchange. The minute you see a sharp rise in it, you better watch out."
      I tend to argue the point, but quietly, and
(10) mostly to myself. Gloria was born and raised in New York; she has come to believe in the stock exchange as the only index of economic health. My perceptions were shaped in South Carolina; and long ago I learned there, as a
(15) waiter in private clubs, to gauge economic flux by the tips people gave. We tend to agree on other matters too, but the thing that gives me most frustration is trying to make her understand why I like country music. Perhaps
(20) it is because she hates the South and has capitulated emotionally to the horror stories told by refugees from down home. Perhaps it is because Gloria is third generation Northern-born. I do not know. What I do know is that,
(25) while the two of us are black, the distance between us is sometimes as great as that between Ibo and Yoruba.

From James Alan McPherson's WHY I LIKE COUNTRY MUSIC, © 1972

2. How do the musical tastes of Gloria and her husband compare?

    (1) They enjoy the same types of music.
    (2) They both dislike bluegrass.
    (3) Only the husband likes hillbilly music.
    (4) Only Gloria enjoys bebop.
    (5) The husband cannot listen to country music.

3. Gloria says that hillbilly music is "like the New York Stock Exchange" (lines 6–7). What is meant by this comparison?

    Her comparison is meant to

    (1) show similarities that are both negative
    (2) give country music a positive association
    (3) associate hillbilly music with prosperity
    (4) imply that stock brokers enjoy country music
    (5) conclude that music affects the stock market

4. The narrator says that "Gloria is third generation Northern-born" (lines 23–24). Why might the author provide this information?

    The author's purpose in providing this information is to

    (1) show that she and her husband have a similar background
    (2) contrast her background with her husband's
    (3) imply that her husband is also from the North
    (4) emphasize her preference for the South
    (5) describe how she appreciates Southern customs

5. Based on the information in the text, how might the author describe the Yoruba and Ibo tribes?

    (1) the beginning and the start
    (2) warm and hot
    (3) girls and women
    (4) night and day
    (5) the moon and the stars

Plot Elements

UNIT 2

① Learn the Skill

The **plot** of the story is made up of the series of events that occur in a story. Authors use specific **plot elements** to tell the events of stories in a particular order. The author sets the scene at the beginning with **exposition**, the background and details of a story.

The story then introduces **complications**, or difficulties, that the people in the story must overcome. Complications are often the result of conflicts between two or more people, or within one person. The complications are most intense at the story's **climax**, which usually comes just before the end. Complications are resolved, happily or unhappily, in the **resolution** at the end of the story.

② Practice the Skill

By mastering the skill of identifying plot elements, you will improve your study and test-taking skills, especially as they relate to the GED Language Arts/Reading Test. Read the excerpt and strategies below. Then answer the question that follows.

A In this story's exposition, a witness is retelling events that set up the story's plot and provide background.

B This news, and how it is explained, presents the story's main plot complication.

WHY DOES MR. HALE GO TO THE HOUSE?

"Well, Mr. Hale," said the county attorney,…"tell just what happened when you came here yesterday morning.…"

"I didn't see or hear anything. I knocked at the door.…

(5) I knocked again, louder, and I thought I heard somebody say, 'Come in.' I wasn't sure—I'm not sure yet. But I opened the door—this door," jerking a hand toward the door by which the two women stood, "and there, in that rocker"—pointing to it—"sat Mrs. Wright.…"

(10) "I thought of Harry and the team outside, so I said, a little sharp, 'Can't I see John?' 'No,' says she—kind of dull like. 'Ain't he home?' says I. Then she looked at me. 'Yes,' says she, 'he's home.' 'Then why can't I see him?' I asked her, out of patience with her now. 'Cause he's dead' says

(15) she, just as quiet and dull—and fell to pleatin' her apron."

From Susan Glaspell's A JURY OF HER PEERS, © 1917

✓ TEST-TAKING TIPS

Think of complications as roadblocks that must be avoided or moved in order for the plot to continue.

1. What complication does the speaker discover at Mrs. Wright's house?

   (1) He finds that Mrs. Wright is ill.
   (2) He learns that John is dead.
   (3) No one can answer the door.
   (4) Mrs. Wright cannot speak.
   (5) John tells him a disturbing story.

Directions: Choose the <u>one best answer</u> to each question.

<u>Questions 2 through 5</u> refer to the following excerpt.

**WHY IS GOODMAN PARKER OUTSIDE
THE WIDOW'S HOUSE?**

"What would you have, Goodman Parker?" cried the widow.

"Lack-a-day, is it you, Mistress Margaret?" replied the innkeeper. "I was afraid it might
(5) be your sister Mary; for I hate to see a young woman in trouble, when I haven't a word of comfort to whisper her."

"For Heaven's sake, what news do you bring?" screamed Margaret.
(10) "Why, there has been an express through the town within this half hour," said Goodman Parker, "traveling from the eastern jurisdiction with letters from the governor and council. He tarried at my house to refresh himself with
(15) a drop and a morsel, and I asked him what tidings on the frontiers. He tells me we had the better in the skirmish you wot of, and that thirteen men reported slain are well and sound, and your husband among them….I judged you
(20) wouldn't mind being broke of your rest, and so I stept over to tell you. Good night."

From Nathaniel Hawthorn's THE WIVES OF THE DEAD, © 1832

2. Goodman Parker is pleased that Margaret answers him instead of Mary because he does not have "a word of comfort" for Mary (lines 6–7). What exposition does this statement give about Mary?

From his statement we can infer that

(1) Goodman Parker wants to see only Mary
(2) Mary and Margaret do not get along
(3) Goodman Parker has good news for Mary
(4) Mary is experiencing difficulty
(5) Margaret will give news to Mary

3. Goodman Parker's speech reveals what complication?

(1) Margaret's husband was reported dead, but he is actually alive.
(2) Mary's husband is dead.
(3) Margaret's husband is dead.
(4) Thirteen men have been killed.
(5) Margaret's husband has returned to her.

4. Margaret screams at Goodman Parker to find out his news (lines 8–9). What might be the author's purpose in delaying Goodman Parker's information?

(1) to show how Mary's problems are resolved
(2) to show that his information is the story's climax
(3) to provide additional exposition
(4) to resolve the conflicts in the plot
(5) to heighten the suspense of the plot

5. Based on the excerpt, what might be one possible conflict between Mary and Margaret?

(1) Goodman Parker's news is revealed to be false.
(2) Mary is pleased with Margaret's good news.
(3) Margaret has received happy news, but Mary remains unhappy.
(4) Both Margaret and Mary will receive happy news.
(5) Margaret and Mary comfort one another in their grief.

Characters

① Learn the Skill

Characters are the fictional people authors create in their stories. Authors bring characters to life by describing their appearances, their thoughts and actions, and other characters' responses to them. On the GED Language Arts/Reading test, you will be asked to analyze the traits and actions of different characters.

② Practice the Skill

By mastering the skill of analyzing characters, you will improve your study and test-taking skills, especially as they relate to the GED Language Arts/Reading Test. Read the excerpt and strategies below. Then answer the question that follows.

Ⓐ Details in the excerpt indicate that Mrs. Whipple acts a particular way around her neighbors. Think about reasons why Mrs. Whipple might act this way.

Ⓑ Here, the author provides both direct and indirect examples of Mrs. Whipple's character traits.

WHAT IS REVEALED ABOUT MRS. WHIPPLE?

Life was very hard for the Whipples. It was hard to feed all the hungry mouths. It was hard to keep the children in flannels during the winter, short as it was: "God knows what would become of us if we lived north,"
(5) they would say: keeping them decently clean was hard. "It looks like our luck won't never let up on us," said Mr. Whipple, but Mrs. Whipple was all for taking what was sent and calling it good, <u>anyhow when the neighbors were in</u>
Ⓐ <u>earshot</u>. "Don't ever let a soul hear us complain," she kept
(10) saying to her husband. <u>She couldn't stand to be pitied.</u>
Ⓑ <u>"No, not if it comes to it that we have to live in a wagon and pick cotton around the country," she said, "nobody's going to get a chance to look down on us</u>."

From Katherine Anne Porter's HE, © 1930

✓ TEST-TAKING TIPS

Look at details that indicate how characters think, move, and respond. Characters may not always mean what they say; these details are the clues about a character's personality.

1. Based on this excerpt, which of the following best describes the character of Mrs. Whipple?

   (1) She loves her children tenderly.
   (2) She gives up easily.
   (3) She is sympathetic to others.
   (4) She is pitiful.
   (5) She is proud.

Directions: Choose the <u>one best answer</u> to each question.

Questions 2 through 6 refer to the following excerpt.

HOW DOES MRS. SLADE VIEW HERSELF?

A few years later, and not many months apart, both ladies lost their husbands….

No doubt, Mrs. Slade reflected, she felt her unemployment more than poor Grace
(5) ever would. It was a big drop from being the wife of Delphin Slade to being his widow. She had always regarded herself (with a certain conjugal pride) as his equal in social gifts, as contributing her full share to the making
(10) of the exceptional couple they were: but the difference after his death was irremediable. As the wife of the famous corporation lawyer, always with an international case or two on hand, every day brought its exciting
(15) and unexpected obligation: the impromptu entertaining of eminent colleagues from abroad, the hurried dashes on legal business to London, Paris or Rome, where the entertaining was so handsomely reciprocated;
(20) the amusement of hearing in her wakes: "What, that handsome woman with the good clothes and the eyes is Mrs. Slade—the Slade's wife! Really! Generally the wives of celebrities are such frumps."
(25) Yes; being the Slade's widow was a dullish business after that.

From Edith Wharton's ROMAN FEVER, © 1934

2. Mrs. Slade recollects her life as the "wife of a famous corporation lawyer" (lines 12–13). What does this tell us about Mrs. Slade?

   Her memories indicate that she

   (1) worked as her husband's partner
   (2) sees Grace as her best friend
   (3) still grieves over her husband's death
   (4) was proud of her social position
   (5) never accompanied her husband on business

3. Which of the following best describes Mrs. Slade?

   (1) confident and materialistic
   (2) thoughtful and quiet
   (3) nervous and edgy
   (4) relaxed and casual
   (5) depressed and grieving

4. The author likely had a reason for writing from Mrs. Slade's perspective. What might this reason be?

   The author probably wanted to portray Mrs. Slade's personality through

   (1) others' opinions
   (2) others' responses to her
   (3) her emotional reactions
   (4) her actions
   (5) her thoughts

5. What is meant by the statement referring to Mrs. Slade that "generally the wives of celebrities are such frumps" (lines 23–24)?

   (1) Mrs. Slade does not dress carefully.
   (2) Mrs. Slade is more important socially than her husband.
   (3) Mrs. Slade is more attractive than most other wives of her social class.
   (4) Mr. Slade requires his wife to dress well.
   (5) Mrs. Slade is not a celebrity.

6. Before her husband's death, Mrs. Slade entertained guests frequently. In present-day terms, how might you describe her position?

   (1) a career woman
   (2) a socialite
   (3) a retiree
   (4) a working mother
   (5) an active volunteer

Motivation

① Learn the Skill

Motivation is the reason that characters act in a particular way or make certain choices. Characters may be motivated by fear, greed, embarrassment, or love of another character. By looking at what characters say, how they act, and how other characters respond, readers can determine why characters make certain decisions. Being able to identify characters' motivations will help you answer questions about why characters behave in a certain way.

② Practice the Skill

By mastering the skill of analyzing character motivation, you will improve your study and test-taking skills, especially as they relate to the GED Language Arts/Reading Test. Read the excerpt and strategies below. Then answer the question that follows.

A Perry Jr.'s mother made a business decision that he obviously does not agree with. Her presentation of the documents to her children shows that she is pleased with the decision she made.

B The daughter Martha calls her mother's action a "vengeful triumph." Based on this, we can tell that the mother had performed an act that she knows will displease her children.

WHY DOES THE MOTHER SELL THE HOUSE?

Some papers their mother had in her purse, that was the occasion. Notarized contracts.…She'd sold Marlcrest…to a developer who planned to bulldoze the house, clear the land, build a subdivision there. Plantation

(5) Oaks, he'd call it. "Here is a copy of the title deed," she said, passing it to Perry Jr. "And you will see, it is properly signed and notarized." He turned it over, held it up to the light, looking for the error that would void the contract. As for the family records and belongings—the *contents* of the

(10) house, she said, leaning toward them from her wheelchair with her hands folded in her lap and high color in her cheeks, savoring (Martha saw) the vengeful triumph of this theft—she'd sold them all to a young man from a southern history museum in Atlanta.

From Pam Durban's SOON, © 1996

☑ TEST-TAKING TIPS

In reading for motivation, look at how other characters respond to an action. These responses can help you figure out the reasons characters acted in a particular way.

1. Based on the excerpt, what is most likely the mother's motivation for selling her family's property?

   (1) to get money for her children
   (2) to preserve her history
   (3) to hurt her children's feelings
   (4) to pay off debts
   (5) to avoid paying taxes

Directions: Choose the <u>one best answer</u> to each question.

<u>Questions 2 through 5</u> refer to the following excerpt.

WHY ARE THE MEN ARGUING?

In the front Shirley was talking to Siggie, the cheese man. Seeing him up there, leaning casually on the counter, Greenspahn felt a quick anger. He walked up the aisle toward
(5) him.

    Siggie saw him coming. "*Shalom*, Jake," he called.

    "I want to talk to you."

    "Is it important, Jake, because I'm in some
(10) terrific hurry. I still got deliveries."

    "What did you leave me?"

    "The same, Jake. The same. A couple pounds blue. Some Swiss. Delicious," he said, smacking his lips.
(15)   "I been getting complaints, Siggie."

    "From the Americans, right? Your average American don't know from cheese. It don't mean nothing." He turned to go.

    "Siggie, where you running?"
(20)   "Jake, I'll be back tomorrow. You can talk to me about it."

    "Now."

    He turned reluctantly. "What's the matter?"

    "You're leaving old stuff. Who's your
(25) wholesaler?"

    "Jake, Jake," he said. "We already been over this. I pick up the returns, don't I?"

    "That's not the point."

    "Have you ever lost a penny account of
(30) me?"

    "Siggie, who's your wholesaler? Where do you get the stuff?"

    "I'm cheaper than the dairy, right? Ain't I cheaper than the dairy? Come on, Jake. What
(35) do you want?"

    "Siggie, don't be a jerk. Who are you talking to? Don't be a jerk. You leave me cheap, crummy cheese, the dairies are ready to throw it away. I get everybody else's returns.
(40) It's old when I get it. Do you think a customer wants a cheese it goes off like a bomb two days after she gets it home? And what about the customers who don't return it? They think I'm gypping them and they don't come back. I
(45) don't want the *schlak* stuff. Give me fresh or I'll take from somebody else."

From Stanley Elkin's CRIERS AND KIBITZERS, KIBITZERS AND CRIERS, © 1962

2. Why does Greenspahn want to talk to Siggie?

    (1) He wants to offer Siggie cheese.
    (2) He wants to sell Siggie cheese.
    (3) Greenspahn thinks Siggie is cheating him.
    (4) Greenspahn intends to complement Siggie.
    (5) Siggie plans to increase his order.

3. Why would a wholesaler be motivated to sell products that are outdated or inferior?

    (1) to maintain a good reputation
    (2) to increase profit
    (3) to please customers
    (4) to expand a base of operations
    (5) to get feedback on a product

4. Siggie states that he cannot talk because he is in "some terrific hurry" (lines 9–10). Why do you think Siggie says he's in a hurry?

    (1) He does not want to talk to Greenspahn.
    (2) He is a very good worker.
    (3) He hates to be late.
    (4) He is helping Shirley.
    (5) He is trying to get a good deal for Greenspahn.

5. What is the most likely reason that Greenspahn is confronting Siggie?

    (1) He wants to continue doing business.
    (2) He is satisfied with Siggie's service.
    (3) His customers have complimented the cheese.
    (4) His sales have increased.
    (5) His customers have complained.

Point of View

1 Learn the Skill

A story is told from a particular **point of view**. It may be told by an **omniscient**, or all-knowing, narrator who knows the thoughts and feelings of all the characters. Or it may be told through a **first-person** narrative. Both of these kinds of writing can affect how a reader receives information about a story. An omniscient point of view lets the reader know what multiple characters are thinking or feeling, while a first-person narrative requires the reader to rely on a single character's perception of events and other characters.

2 Practice the Skill

By mastering the skill of determining point of view, you will improve your study and test-taking skills, especially as they relate to the GED Language Arts/Reading Test. Read the excerpt and strategies below. Then answer the question that follows.

A The pronoun *her* indicates that this story is told from an omniscient point of view. This narrator informs readers about Connie's thoughts and feelings.

B The omniscient narrator also has access to the thoughts and feelings of Connie's mother, who "noticed everything."

WHAT DOES THIS PASSAGE REVEAL ABOUT CONNIE?

Her name was Connie. She was fifteen and she had a quick nervous giggling habit of craning her neck to glance into mirrors, or <u>checking other people's faces to</u> **A** <u>make sure her own was all right</u>. Her mother, who <u>noticed</u> (5) <u>everything and knew everything and who hadn't much</u> **B** <u>reason any longer to look at her own face</u>, always scolded Connie about it. "Stop gawking at yourself, who are you? You think you're so pretty?" she would say. Connie would raise her eyebrows at those familiar complaints and look (10) right through her mother, into a shadowy vision of herself as she was right at that moment: she knew she was pretty and that was everything.

From Joyce Carol Oates' WHERE ARE YOU GOING, WHERE HAVE YOU BEEN?, © 1967

✓ TEST-TAKING TIPS

When analyzing point of view, look closely at which pronouns are used. The pronouns *I* and *we* indicate a first-person point of view, while *he* and *she* show that an omniscient narrator is telling the story.

1. The narrator of the passage depicts an exchange between a mother and daughter. How is this exchange described?

In this excerpt, the narrator

(1) depicts only the mother's thoughts
(2) describes the daughter's actions, but not her thoughts
(3) reveals the thoughts and actions of both characters
(4) does not explain the mother's feelings
(5) does not include the daughter's feelings

Directions: Choose the <u>one best answer</u> to each question.

<u>Questions 2 through 5</u> refer to the following excerpt.

WHAT DO WE LEARN ABOUT THE CHARACTERS IN THIS EXCERPT?

During my holidays from school, I was allowed to stay in bed until long after my father had gone to work. He left our house every weekday at the stroke of seven by the Anglican

(5) church bell. I would lie in bed awake, and I could hear all the sounds my parents made as they prepared for the day ahead. As my mother made my father his breakfast, my father would shave, using his shaving brush that had an

(10) ivory handle and a razor that matched; then he would step outside to the little shed he had built for us as a bathroom, to quickly bathe in water that he had instructed my mother to leave outside overnight in the dew. That way,

(15) the water would be very cold, and he believed that cold water strengthened his back. If I had been a boy, I would have gotten the same treatment, but since I was a girl, and on top of that went to school only with other girls, my

(20) mother would always add some hot water to my bathwater to take off the chill. On Sunday afternoons, while I was in Sunday school, my father took a hot bath; the tub was half filled with plain water, and then my mother would

(25) add a large caldronful of water in which she had just boiled some bark and leaves from a bay-leaf tree. The bark and leaves were there for no reason other than that he liked the smell. He would then spend hours lying in this

(30) bath, studying his pool coupons or drawing examples of pieces of furniture he planned to make. When I came home from Sunday school, we would sit down to our Sunday dinner.

From Jamaica Kincaid's THE CIRCLING HAND, © 1985

2. From whose point of view is the passage told?

  (1) the mother and father's
  (2) the father's
  (3) the mother's
  (4) the girl's
  (5) an omniscient narrator's

3. The girl in the excerpt says that "I would lie in bed awake, and I could hear all the sounds my parents made as they prepared for the day ahead" (lines 5–7). What does the pronoun "I" indicate?

  (1) the story is a first-person account
  (2) an omniscient narrator will tell the story
  (3) all the mother's thoughts will be revealed
  (4) the story will be told from the parents' point of view
  (5) readers will not have access to the girl's feelings

4. What might be the author's purpose in presenting this point of view?

  (1) to provide insight into a family's feelings
  (2) to analyze a father's bathing habits
  (3) to reveal a mother's hidden resentment
  (4) to explain what all young girls think about their parents
  (5) to present the thoughts and feelings of one young girl

5. What does the daughter's account of her parents most resemble?

  (1) a journalist's objective account of an event
  (2) a diary writer explaining daily events
  (3) a person writing a poem to express feelings
  (4) a movie reviewer analyzing a film
  (5) a mystery writer giving clues about a crime

UNIT 2

Theme

① Learn the Skill

A story's **theme** is the insight or general idea that the author shares with readers. A theme does not sum up a story's plot. Instead, it gives a lesson or a moral about human nature. For example, the plot of the fairy tale *Cinderella* is about a poor girl who marries a prince. Its theme, however, might be stated as "keep hoping for better days." Themes are not often stated directly, so readers must use clues from the text to discover the implied message.

② Practice the Skill

By mastering the skill of identifying a story's theme, you will improve your study and test-taking skills, especially as they relate to the GED Language Arts/Reading Test. Read the excerpt and strategies below. Then answer the question that follows.

WHAT IS THE WOMAN HIDING?

A The narrator's speech indicates that the mother "covers up" an important part of her personality. Think about how this deception plays a role in the story's theme.

B The story indicates that the mother effectively hides her feelings from everyone except those that matter most: her children.

There was a woman who was beautiful, who started with all the advantages, yet she had no luck.…She had bonny [beautiful] children, yet she felt they had been thrust upon her, and she could not love them. They looked at her
(5) coldly, as if they were finding fault with her. And hurriedly she felt she must cover up some fault in herself. Yet what it was that she must cover up she never knew. Nevertheless, when her children were present, she always felt the center of her heart go hard. This troubled her, and in her manner
(10) she was all the more gentle and anxious for her children, as if she loved them very much. Only she herself knew that at the center of her heart was a hard little place that could not feel love, no, not for anybody. Everybody else said of her: "She is such a good mother. She adores her
(15) children." Only she herself, and her children themselves, knew it was not so. They read it in each other's eyes.

From D. H. Lawrence's THE ROCKING HORSE WINNER, © 1926

▶ MAKING ASSUMPTIONS

The excerpt says the woman has a "hard little place" in her heart. We can assume that an inability to love causes a great deal of pain for her family.

1. Which of the following sentences best states the theme of this excerpt?

   (1) Truly deceptive people can hide their feelings.
   (2) Children love their parents despite everything.
   (3) Nothing can come between parents and their children.
   (4) True feelings cannot be disguised.
   (5) A mother's love always endures.

Directions: Choose the <u>one best answer</u> to each question.

<u>Questions 2 through 6</u> refer to the following excerpt.

WHY IS DONALD UPSET?

     In a way, Donald's absences are a fine arrangement, even considerate. He is sparing them his darkest moods, when he can't cope with his memories of Vietnam. Vietnam had
(5) never seemed such a meaningful fact until a couple of years ago, when he grew depressed and moody....He isn't really working regularly at the strip mines. He is mostly just hanging around there, watching the land being scraped
(10) away, trees coming down, bushes flung in the air. Sometimes he operates a steam shovel, and when he comes home his clothes are filled with the clay and it is caked on his shoes. The clay is the color of butterscotch pudding.
(15)   At first, he tried to explain to Jeannette. He said, "If we could have had tanks over there as big as Big Bertha, we wouldn't have lost the war. Strip mining is just like what we were doing over there. We were stripping off the top.
(20) The topsoil is like the culture and the people, the best part of the land and the country. America was just stripping off the top, the best. We ruined it. Here, at least the coal companies have to plant vetch and loblolly pines and all
(25) kinds of trees and bushes. If we'd done that in Vietnam, maybe we'd have left that country in better shape."

From Bobbie Ann Mason's BIG BERTHA STORIES, © 1988

2. Which of the following best states the theme of this excerpt?

   (1) Many men fought in the Vietnam War.
   (2) The wounds of war always heal.
   (3) War disrupts people deeply.
   (4) Jeannette does not understand war.
   (5) Strip mining destroys the countryside.

3. Why is Donald depressed and moody?

   (1) He does not like working at the strip mines.
   (2) His experience in Vietnam still haunts him.
   (3) He does not like living with his family.
   (4) His job is unsatisfying.
   (5) He cannot explain his feelings to Jeannette.

4. Donald says that "We were stripping off the top. The topsoil is like the culture and the people…" (lines 19–20). What might this indicate?

His comparison indicates that

   (1) both activities are destructive
   (2) both activities are productive
   (3) only strip mining damages a culture
   (4) neither strip mining nor war damage a culture
   (5) soldiers tried to heal Vietnamese people

5. Which word best describes the way Donald feels in this excerpt?

   (1) sensitive
   (2) compassionate
   (3) perplexed
   (4) haunted
   (5) upbeat

6. With which of the following statements would Donald probably agree?

   (1) War is beneficial to society.
   (2) Men should work hard for their families.
   (3) Big industry is vital to America's economy.
   (4) Families always understand soldiers' experiences.
   (5) If you break something, you should fix it.

Setting

① Learn the Skill

A story's **setting** is the time when and place where events happen. Authors develop a setting through details such as describing scenery, the items found in a room, or characters' clothing and accents. The setting adds depth and complexity to a tale. A story that takes place in the middle of the night, for example, is likely to have a different feel to it than a story set in a high school cafeteria.

② Practice the Skill

By mastering the skill of understanding setting, you will improve your study and test-taking skills, especially as they relate to the GED Language Arts/Reading Test. Read the excerpt and strategies below. Then answer the question that follows.

A The author provides many setting details for the reader, such as the elaborate decorations and presents for the guests.

B The details in the setting can affect the feeling of a story. Here, the gifts on the table are silly and funny. The setting helps create a lighthearted feeling for the story.

WHAT DOES THE RESTAURANT LOOK LIKE?

A The restaurant was quite a pretty place. Every table had a mammoth floral display, as big as a tree, in the center, and there were little place cards and gifts at each place. My card said "Guest of Mr. Stosz"—I was

(5) seated next to the place card of "Stash Stosz"—and my gift was selected by someone who must have known my situation as well as my vocation: it was a large fake diamond engagement-and-wedding-ring set. Stash got a

B set of tattoos, water-soluble, and toy motorcycle—Stash

(10) owned a motorcycle—which, when he wound it up, zipped across the table and fell over. Other artists received Etch A Sketch kits, voodoo dolls, exploding cigars,…and their signatures made into rubber stamps.

From Tama Janowitz's PHYSICS, © 1985

☑ TEST-TAKING TIPS

You may want to create a chart to organize categories of setting details.

Place	a big fancy restaurant
Time Period	the present
Important Details	elaborate, expensive place cards and gifts

1. Based on the details provided, what can you conclude about the setting?

(1) The restaurant is small and intimate.
(2) The restaurant is closed for the day.
(3) The restaurant is not popular.
(4) The restaurant is decorated for a party.
(5) The restaurant serves excellent food.

UNIT 2

Directions: Choose the <u>one best answer</u> to each question.

<u>Questions 2 through 5</u> refer to the following excerpt.

HOW DOES THE SETTING AFFECT THE HAWK?

Hook, the Hawks' child, was hatched in a dry spring among the oaks beside the seasonal river, and was struck from the nest early. In the drought his single-willed parents
(5) had to extend their hunting ground by more than twice. The range became too great for them to wish to return and feed Hook, and when they had lost interest in each other they drove Hook down into the sand and brush
(10) and went back to solitary courses over the bleaching hills.
Unable to fly yet, Hook crept over the ground, challenging all large movements with recoiled head, erected rudimentary wings,
(15) and the small rasp of his clattering beak. It was during this time of abysmal ignorance and continual fear that his eyes took on the first quality of hawk, that of being wide, alert and challenging. He dwelt, because of his
(20) helplessness, among the rattling brush which grew between the oaks and the river.
Two spacious sounds environed Hook at this time. One was the great rustle of the slopes of yellowed wild wheat, with over it the
(25) chattering rustle of the leaves of the California oaks. The other was the distant whisper of the foaming edge of the Pacific, punctuated by the hollow shoring of the waves.

From Walter Van Tilburg Clark's HOOK, © 1940

2. According to the details in the excerpt, where does the hawk live?

   (1) on the beach
   (2) in the high prairie
   (3) on an island
   (4) in a mountain range
   (5) near the Pacific Ocean

3. In the passage, Hook's parents have to "extend their hunting ground" because of a drought (line 5). How might human parents deal with this difficulty?

   They might

   (1) buy food at discount stores
   (2) accept help from a food bank
   (3) move to a new town to find work
   (4) enroll a child in a different school
   (5) apply for a housing subsidy

4. Hook lives "among the rattling brush" (line 20). What is the author's purpose in describing where the hawk lives?

   The purpose is to

   (1) show the beauty of the landscape
   (2) emphasize the difficulty of the hawk's existence
   (3) illustrate humans' impact on the countryside
   (4) depict the ideal environment for hawks
   (5) record the effects of a drought

5. Because of a drought, Hook's parents move him from the nest early, driving him "down into the sand and brush" (line 9). What do their actions imply about the story's setting?

   (1) The hawks expect Hook to feed on wild wheat.
   (2) The brush region is the perfect place for young hawks.
   (3) The countryside is harsh but beautiful.
   (4) Birds must change their lifestyles significantly to adapt to weather patterns.
   (5) Hook can drink from the Pacific Ocean.

Tone

Fiction

① Learn the Skill

When discussing short stories, the term **tone** means the feeling of the story. The tone can be, for example, happy, sad, condescending, encouraging, formal, or familiar. A story's tone expresses the author's attitude about the subject. Word choices and other details let readers know, for example, if the author is treating a subject seriously or is approaching it with irony or humor. A story's characters, setting, and some plot elements can affect the tone of the story.

② Practice the Skill

By being able to interpret the tone of a literary work, you will improve your study and test-taking skills, especially as they relate to the GED Language Arts/Reading Test. Read the excerpt and strategies below. Then answer the question that follows.

WHAT DID THE YOUNG MAN DO LAST NIGHT?

A The man's tone in the paragraph indicates that he does not actually feel so good.

"Not feeling so well today?" she asked.
"Oh, I'm great," he said. "Corking, I am. Know what time I got up? Four o'clock this afternoon, sharp. I kept trying to make it, and every time I took my head off the pillow, it would roll under the (5) bed. This isn't my head I've got on now. I think this is something that used to belong to Walt Whitman. Oh, dear, oh, dear, oh, dear.
"Do you think maybe a drink would make you feel better?" she said.

B The woman's tone indicates that she is trying to make the man feel better about the events of the previous night. Think about how tone might help you understand the characters' interactions.

"The hair of the mastiff that bit me?" he said. "Oh, no, thank (10) you. Please never speak of anything like that again. I'm through. I'm all, all through. Look at that hand; steady as a humming-bird. Tell me, was I very terrible last night?"
"Oh, goodness," she said, "everybody was feeling pretty high [good]. You were all right."

From Dorothy Parker's YOU WERE PERFECTLY FINE, © 1930

USING LOGIC

When reading for tone, determine whether characters' statements match the manner in which they are delivered. Serious statements delivered in a casual way tell readers the author is likely aiming for a particular effect.

1. The young man in the story is experiencing distress. How might you describe the author's tone in describing the young man?

   (1) uncaring
   (2) bitter
   (3) concerned
   (4) humorous
   (5) formal

Apply the Skill

Directions: Choose the <u>one best answer</u> to each question.

<u>Questions 2 through 6</u> refer to the following excerpt.

HOW DOES THE FULL MOON AFFECT PEOPLE?

Up from the skeleton stone walls, up from the rotting floor boards and the solid hand-hewn beams of oak of the pre-war cotton factory, dusk came. Up from the dusk the full
(5) moon came. Glowing like a fired pine-knot it illuminated the great door and soft showered the Negro shanties aligned along the single street of factory town. The full moon in the great door was an omen. Negro women
(10) improvised songs against its spell….

A strange stir was in her [Louisa]. Indolently she tried to fix upon Bob or Tom as the cause of it….Separately there was no unusual significance to either one. But for
(15) some reason they jumbled when her eyes gazed vacantly at the rising moon. And from the jumble came the stir that was strangely within her. Her lips trembled. The slow rhythm of her song grew agitant and restless. Rusty
(20) black and tan spotted hounds, lying in the dark corners of porches or prowling around back yards, put their noses in the air and caught its tremor. They began to plaintively yelp and howl. Chickens woke up, and cackled.
(25) Intermittently, all over the country-side dogs barked and roosters crowed as if heralding a weird dawn or some ungodly awakening. The women sang lustily. Their songs were cottonwads to stop their ears. Louisa came
(30) down into factory town and sank wearily upon the step before her home. The moon was rising towards a thick cloud-bank that soon would hide it.

From Jean Toomer's BLOOD-BURNING MOON, © 1923

2. Which of the following best describes the tone of the excerpt?

   (1) humorous
   (2) cheerful
   (3) calm
   (4) threatening
   (5) envious

3. Dogs and chickens are "heralding a weird dawn or some ungodly awakening" (lines 26–27). What does the animals' behavior imply?

   The behavior implies

   (1) the evening is completely normal
   (2) some misfortune is about to take place
   (3) the sun is about to rise
   (4) the moon is going down
   (5) the weather is unusual

4. In the passage, a rising moon is an "omen" (line 9). What other type of writing might include an ominous moon?

   (1) a news story
   (2) a fairy tale
   (3) a sports account
   (4) a humorous piece
   (5) a mystery tale

5. In the passage, what is the women's response to the full moon?

   (1) They sing to guard against it.
   (2) They turn their heads and refuse to see it.
   (3) They admire it.
   (4) They howl at it.
   (5) They watch it from their porches.

6. Louisa has "agitant and restless" feelings about Bob and Tom (line 19). What do her emotions suggest?

   They suggest that

   (1) she loves only Bob
   (2) she loves Bob, but not Tom
   (3) she cares for both characters
   (4) neither of the men care for her
   (5) she has no one to love

UNIT 2

Figurative Language

1 Learn the Skill

Authors use **figurative language**, such as **metaphors** and **similes**, to paint vivid pictures and create memorable images. A metaphor states that one thing is like another: *the baby's face was a rose*. A simile makes this comparison using the words *like, as*, or *similar to*: *the burned cake was* <u>*like*</u> *a brick*. Other types of figurative language include **hyperbole**, or extreme exaggeration, and **personification**, in which the author gives human qualities to animals or inanimate objects. Words such as *boom* and *splash* reflect the sounds they describe; they are examples of **onomatopoeia**.

2 Practice the Skill

By mastering the skill of identifying figurative language, you will improve your study and test-taking skills, especially as they relate to the GED Language Arts/Reading Test. Read the excerpt and strategies below. Then answer the question that follows.

A In this excerpt, the calf speaks to his mother just as a human child would.

B Numerous calves ask questions of the mother cow. Her patient response resembles that of a human mother.

WHAT HAPPENS TO ALL THE CATTLE?

A <u>The calf ran up the hill as fast as he could and stopped sharp. "Mama!" he cried, all out of breath</u>. "What is it! What are they *doing*! Where are they *going*?"
Other spring calves came galloping too.
(5) They all were looking up at her and awaiting her explanation, but she looked out over their excited eyes. As she waited the mysterious and majestic thing they had never seen before, her own eyes became even more **B** than ordinarily still, and <u>during the considerable moment
(10) before she answered, she scarcely heard their urgent questioning</u>.

From James Agee's A MOTHER'S TALE, © 1952

☑ TEST-TAKING TIPS

Authors use figurative language to help readers think about a subject in a different way. Look for comparisons that seem unusual or striking.

1. Which type of figurative language is used in this excerpt?

    (1) simile
    (2) metaphor
    (3) hyperbole
    (4) personification
    (5) onomatopoeia

③ Apply the Skill

<u>Directions</u>: Choose the <u>one best answer</u> to each question.

<u>Questions 2 through 5</u> refer to the following excerpt.

HOW DOES PAIN AFFECT THE PATIENT?

Blunderer that he was, Dr. Nicholas was an honorable enemy, not like the demon, pain, which sulked in a thousand guises within her head, and which often she recklessly willed
(5) to attack her and then drove back in terror. After the rout, sweat streamed from her face and soaked the neck of the coarse hospital shirt. To be sure, it came usually of its own accord, running like a wild fire through all the
(10) convolutions [complications] to fill with flame the small sockets and ravines and then, at last, to withdraw, leaving behind a throbbing and an echo. On these occasions, she was as helpless as a tree in the wind. But at other
(15) times when, by closing her eyes and rolling up the eyeballs in such a way that she fancied she looked directly on the place where her brain was, the pain woke sluggishly and came toward her at a snail's pace. Then, bit by bit,
(20) it gained speed. Sometimes it faltered back, subsided altogether, and then it rushed like a tidal wave driven by a hurricane, lashing and roaring until she lifted her hands from the counterpane, crushed her broken teeth into
(25) her swollen lip, stared in panic at the soothing walls with her ruby eyes, stretched out her legs until she felt their bones must snap. Each cove, each narrow inlet, every living bay was flooded and the frail brain, a little hat-shaped boat, was
(30) washed from its mooring and set adrift. The skull was as vast as the world and the brain was as small as a seashell.

From Jean Stafford's THE INTERIOR CASTLE, © 1969

2. The character is described as being "as helpless as a tree in the wind" (line 14). What type of figurative language is included in this description?

It is an example of

(1) onomatopoeia
(2) metaphor
(3) simile
(4) hyperbole
(5) personification

3. Why is pain compared to a wild fire (line 9)?

(1) to reveal its heat
(2) to indicate its speed
(3) to prove its intensity
(4) to show its size
(5) to illustrate its depth

4. Which of the following describes the writing of this excerpt?

It contains

(1) similes
(2) short sentences
(3) onomatopoeia
(4) metaphors
(5) several vivid characters

5. Which part of the speaker's body is compared to a seashell?

(1) the skull
(2) the legs
(3) the teeth
(4) the eyeballs
(5) the brain

Symbols and Imagery

① Learn the Skill

A **symbol** is another type of figurative language. Symbols are people, places, or things that stand for a larger idea. For example, a country's flag is a symbol that represents that country. In stories, characters' feelings or other attributes may be represented by a symbol. Symbols are often repeated throughout the text. **Imagery** is a type of figurative language that appeals to the reader's senses of taste, smell, vision, hearing, or touch. Images, like symbols, help readers understand important ideas.

② Practice the Skill

By mastering the skill of identifying symbols and images, you will improve your study and test-taking skills, especially as they relate to the GED Language Arts/Reading Test. Read the excerpt and strategies below. Then answer the question that follows.

WHAT DOES THE SPEAKER NOT LIKE ABOUT THE OLD MAN?

A The old man did not actually have an eye from a vulture. This imagery gives you an idea of how the eye affected the speaker.

B Notice that the speaker is willing to go to drastic lengths to get rid of the eye.

It is impossible to say how first the idea entered my brain; but, once conceived, it haunted me day and night. Object there was none. Passion there was none. I loved the old man. He had never wronged me. He had never
(5) given me insult. For his gold I had no desire. I think it was his eye!—yes, it was this! He had the eye of a vulture—a pale blue eye, with a film over it. Whenever it fell up on me, my blood ran cold; and so, by degrees—very gradually—I made up my mind to take the life of the old
(10) man, and thus rid myself of the eye forever.

From Edgar Allan Poe's THE TELL-TALE HEART, © 1893

USING LOGIC

The speaker states that even though he loves the old man, he is so haunted by the blue eye that he feels he must kill the old man. Think of what the eye might symbolize to the speaker.

1. Which of the following does the eye mentioned in the excerpt most likely symbolize to the speaker?

   (1) something that he cannot have
   (2) something that angers him
   (3) something that he loves
   (4) an idea that was stolen from him
   (5) his hatred of the color blue

Directions: Choose the one best answer to each question.

Questions 2 through 5 refer to the following excerpt.

WHY IS THE AIRPLANE SO EXCITING?

We heard the plane come over at noon, roaring through the radio news, and we were sure it was going to hit the house, so we all ran into the yard. We saw it come in over the
(5) treetops, all red and silver, the first close-up plane I ever saw. Mrs. Peebles screamed.

"Crash landing," their little boy said. Joey was his name.

"It's okay," said Dr. Peebles. "He knows
(10) what he's doing." Dr. Peebles was only an animal doctor, but had a calming way of talking, like any doctor.

This was my first job—working for Dr. and Mrs. Peebles, who had bought an old house
(15) out on the Fifth Line, about five miles out of town. It was just when the trend was starting of town people buying up old farms, not to work them but to live on them.

We watched the plane land across the
(20) road, where the fairgrounds used to be. It did make a good landing field, nice and level for the old race track, and the barns and display sheds torn down now for scrap lumber so there was nothing in the way. Even the old
(25) grandstand bays had burned.

"All right," said Mrs. Peebles, snappy as she always was when she got over her nerves. "Let's go back in the house. Let's not stand here gawking like a set of farmers."

From Alice Munro's HOW I MET MY HUSBAND, © 1974

2. What does the excerpt suggest about the noise of the airplane?

The noise

(1) is pleasant
(2) hardly attracts attention
(3) is quieter than most planes
(4) is loud
(5) keeps people from sleeping

3. Based on the excerpt, what might the appearance of the plane symbolize?

(1) the excitement of something new
(2) the changing of the weather
(3) the arrival of the fair
(4) the destruction of the fairgrounds
(5) the end of technology

4. Which of the following might be most similar to the appearance of the plane?

(1) The sight of a bus leaving a station.
(2) The smell of a car's exhaust.
(3) The feel of a horse's warm nose.
(4) The sight of a circus train arriving in town.
(5) The sound of a taxi honking its horn.

5. The speaker describes the old fairgrounds with "display sheds torn down now for scrap lumber so there was nothing in the way" (lines 22–24). How might the image of the old fairgrounds be described?

(1) disappointed
(2) weary
(3) matter-of-fact
(4) grieving
(5) cheerful

Make Inferences

① Learn the Skill

As you learned in Unit 1, authors do not always explain all plot elements directly. Sometimes, readers must **make inferences**, or educated guesses based on suggestions and clues found in the text. When readers make an inference, they combine what they know about a subject with the information found in the text. Then they make a reasonable guess about what the author intends.

② Practice the Skill

By mastering the skill of making inferences, you will improve your study and test-taking skills, especially as they relate to the GED Language Arts/Reading Test. Read the excerpt and strategies below. Then answer the question that follows.

A The reader can infer that the speaker has endured problems in the past.

B From this and the rest of the passage, you can infer that Charlie has gotten into trouble because of his drinking in the past.

WHAT DOES CHARLIE WANT?

A He knew that now he would have to take a beating. It would last an hour or two hours, and it would be difficult, but if he modulated his inevitable resentment to the chastened attitude of the reformed sinner, he might win his
(5) point in the end.

Keep your temper, he told himself. You don't want to be justified. You want Honoria.

Lincoln spoke first: "We've been talking it over ever since we got your letter last month. We're happy to have
(10) Honoria here. She's a dear little thing, and we're glad to be able to help her, but of course that isn't the question—"

B Marion interrupted suddenly. "How long are you going to stay sober, Charlie?" she asked.

"Permanently, I hope."

From F. Scott Fitzgerald's BABYLON REVISITED, © 1959

☑ TEST-TAKING TIPS

Look for evidence of characters referring to events that have happened in the past. These clues can help explain conflicts set in the present.

1. What does Marion's sudden interruption reveal about her feelings toward Charlie?

(1) She respects his judgment.
(2) She wants him to raise his daughter, Honoria.
(3) She admires him.
(4) She scorns him.
(5) She wants to help him.

Directions: Choose the <u>one best answer</u> to each question.

<u>Questions 2 through 6</u> refer to the following excerpt.

WHAT IS WRONG WITH OLE ANDERSON?

Nick opened the door and went into the room. Ole Anderson was lying on the bed with all his clothes on. He had been a heavyweight prizefighter and he was too long for the bed.
(5) He lay with his head on two pillows. He did not look at Nick.

"What was it?" he asked.

"I was up at Henry's," Nick said, "and two fellows came in and tied up me and the cook,
(10) and they said they were going to kill you."

It sounded silly when he said it. Ole Anderson said nothing.

"They put us out in the kitchen," Nick went on. "They were going to shoot you when you
(15) came in to supper."

Ole Anderson looked at the wall and did not say anything.

"George thought I better come and tell you about it."
(20) "There isn't anything I can do about it," Ole Anderson said.

"I'll tell you what they were like."

"I don't want to know what they were like," Ole Anderson said. He looked at the wall.
(25) "Thanks for coming to tell me about it."

"That's all right."

Nick looked at the big man lying on the bed.

"Don't you want me to go and see the
(30) police?"

"No," Ole Anderson said. "That wouldn't do any good."

"Isn't there something I could do?"

"No, there ain't anything to do."
(35) "Maybe it was just a bluff."

"No. It ain't just a bluff."

From Ernest Hemingway's THE KILLERS, © 1927

2. Based on the details in the excerpt, which of the following can we infer about Nick?

(1) He is in danger.
(2) He has come to warn Ole Anderson.
(3) He is afraid of Ole Anderson.
(4) He is threatening Ole Anderson.
(5) He is a heavyweight prizefighter.

3. Ole Anderson "looked at the wall and did not say anything" (lines 16–17). What can readers infer based on this description?

Anderson

(1) is too tired to respond
(2) knows that Nick can save him
(3) believes he is doomed
(4) is hysterical
(5) has another plan

4. Nick warns Ole Anderson about the two men. Which of the following is most like this situation?

(1) forwarding a concerning e-mail to a friend
(2) breaking a secret code
(3) calling to congratulate a winner
(4) writing a letter to a sick friend
(5) sneaking a cell key to a prisoner

5. Ole Anderson says that "It ain't just a bluff" (line 36). What does his matter-of-fact tone imply?

His tone implies that he

(1) is shocked by the news
(2) knows he cannot be helped
(3) does not want to frighten Nick
(4) is friends with the police
(5) is confident of his escape

6. Nick offers to go see the police or describe the men. What does his behavior indicate?

His behavior indicates that

(1) Ole Anderson is his best friend
(2) the cook at Henry's has been hurt
(3) Ole Anderson has put people in danger
(4) the police are dishonest
(5) he wants to help Ole Anderson

UNIT 2

Draw Conclusions

① Learn the Skill

As you learned in Unit 1, **drawing conclusions** is like solving a mystery. As a reader, you gather facts from your reading, combine it with what you know about the topic, and draw a conclusion about the significance of those facts. By drawing conclusions, readers discover connections between events and ideas as they read.

② Practice the Skill

By mastering the skill of drawing conclusions, you will improve your study and test-taking skills, especially as they relate to the GED Language Arts/Reading Test. Read the excerpt and strategies below. Then answer the question that follows.

A Laird is in a wheelchair, and he is covered with blankets. What might the details indicate?

B The fact that "people who haven't seen him for a while" are shocked by Laird's appearance indicates that his illness is having a dramatic effect on him.

WHAT IS WRONG WITH LAIRD?

Her son wanted to talk again, suddenly. During the days, he still brooded, scowling at the swimming pool from the vantage point of his wheelchair, where he sat covered with blankets despite the summer heat….After he was

(5) asleep, Janet would run through the conversations in her mind, and realize what it was she wished she had said.…

A month earlier, after a particular long and grueling visit with a friend who'd come up on the train from New York, Laird had declared a new policy: no visitors, no telephone

(10) calls. She didn't blame him. People who hadn't seen him for a while were often shocked to tears by his appearance, and, rather than have them cheer him up, he felt obliged to comfort them.

From Alice Elliott Dark's IN THE GLOAMING, © 1994

✓ TEST-TAKING TIPS

Adding together details like "blankets despite the summer heat" and "people…were shocked by his appearance" let you know that Laird is very sick, even though the author never explicitly states this information.

1. Which of the following conclusions most accurately sums up the general situation described in the excerpt?

   (1) Laird is being treated for a rare disease.
   (2) Laird is indifferent about his medical treatment.
   (3) Janet has little background in current medicine.
   (4) Janet watches television news programs.
   (5) Janet misses her friends coming to visit.

Directions: Choose the one best answer to each question.

Questions 2 through 5 refer to the following excerpt.

WHAT IS MRS. WILSON'S NEWS?

She wondered how many times a week
he had to do this. Plenty, no doubt. At least
every day. Maybe twice…three times. Maybe,
on a big day, five times. It was the ultimate bad
(5) news, and he delivered it dryly, like Sergeant
Joe Friday. He was a young man, but his was
a tough business and he had gone freeze-
dried already. Hey, the bad news wasn't really
a surprise! She…*knew*. Of course, you always
(10) hope for the best. She heard but she didn't
hear.
    "What?" she offered timidly. She had
hoped...for better. Geez! Give me a break!
What was he saying? Breast and uterus?
(15) Double trouble! She *knew* it would be the
uterus. There had been the discharge. The
bloating, the cramps. The fatigue. But it was
common and easily curable provided you got
it at stage one. Eighty percent cure. But the
(20) breast—that one came out of the blue and
that could be really tricky—that was fifty-fifty.
Strip out the lymph nodes down your arm and
guaranteed chemo. God! Chemo. The worst
thing in the world. Good-bye hair—there'd be
(25) scarves, wigs, a prosthetic breast, crying your
heart out in "support" groups. Et cetera.
    "Mrs. Wilson?" The voice seemed to come
out of a can. Now the truth was revealed and
all was out in the open. Yet how—tell me
(30) this—how would it ever be possible to have a
life again? The voice from the can had chilled
her. To the core.

From Thom Jones's I WANT TO LIVE!, © 1993

2. Based on the evidence in the text, to what does "the voice...out of a can" (lines 27–28) belong?

    The voice belongs to

    (1) a recorded message
    (2) an answering machine
    (3) a movie character
    (4) a doctor
    (5) the speaker's imagination

3. Based on the tone of the excerpt, what could readers conclude about the speaker?

    (1) She is not sympathetic to those around her.
    (2) She typically over-reacts.
    (3) She takes things too seriously.
    (4) She hates Sergeant Joe Friday.
    (5) She has a sense of humor.

4. Based on the evidence in the excerpt, what is "the ultimate bad news" (lines 4–5)?

    The speaker is told

    (1) her child is ill
    (2) she has been fired
    (3) she has cancer
    (4) she is bankrupt
    (5) she has failed a test

5. Which of the following examples is most like the situation described in the excerpt?

    A character is told that a

    (1) letter in the mail indicates she has won the lottery
    (2) letter in the mail says she has failed a test
    (3) newspaper story announces a candidate's victory
    (4) doctor has announced a cure for a terminal disease
    (5) student masters a grueling course

Apply Ideas

1 Learn the Skill

You have practiced making inferences (Lesson 13), and used that information to draw conclusions (Lesson 14). By gathering facts and thinking of reasonable explanations for those facts, you are **applying ideas** that can help you determine or predict unrelated events. For example, when you determine major elements of a character's personality, you can predict how he or she will act in a different situation. Applying ideas to a text can help you better understand the text as a whole.

2 Practice the Skill

By mastering the skill of applying ideas, you will improve your study and test-taking skills, especially as they relate to the GED Language Arts/Reading Test. Read the excerpt and strategies below. Then answer the question that follows.

A The music has a particular effect on Paul. At first, the music appears to give him a kind of joy that he does not otherwise have.

B Paul's "struggl[ing]" spirit indicates that he may feel inhibited in his daily life.

HOW DOES THE SYMPHONY AFFECT PAUL?

A When the symphony began Paul sank into one of the rear seats with a long sigh of relief, and lost himself as he had done before the Rico. It was not that symphonies, as such, meant anything in particular to Paul, but the first

(5) sign of the instruments seemed to free some hilarious and potent spirit within him; something that struggled there like

B the genie in the bottle found by the Arab fisherman. He felt a sudden zest of life; the lights danced before his eyes and the concert hall blazed into unimaginable splendor.

(10) When the soprano soloist came on, Paul forgot even the nastiness of his teacher's being there and gave himself up to the peculiar stimulus such personages always had for him.

From Willa Cather's PAUL'S CASE, © 1905

💡 **USING LOGIC**

Consider how the character would react in a different set of circumstances. A character would probably act consistently, with the same personality traits. Use logic to imagine how these traits might be acted out in a different situation.

1. Based on his behavior in the excerpt, what can you infer about Paul?

   (1) He is great friends with his teacher.
   (2) He goes to the symphony daily.
   (3) He knows the soprano soloist.
   (4) He is deeply moved by the symphony.
   (5) He is a musician.

Directions: Choose the <u>one best answer</u> to each question.

<u>Questions 2 through 5</u> refer to the following excerpt.

WHAT MAKES LEO LOSE HIS TEMPER?

People born into the tradition of English country life are accustomed to eccentric owls. Mrs. Leslie and her daughter Belinda accepted the owl with vague acknowledging smiles. Her
(5) son-in-law, Leo Cooper, a Londoner whose contacts with nature had been made at the very expensive pleasure resorts patronized by his very rich parents, found midday hoots disconcerting, and almost said so. But did not,
(10) as he was just then in a temper and wholly engaged in not showing it.

He was in a temper for several reasons, all eminently adequate. For one thing,...impelled by the nervous appetite of frustration he had
(15) eaten a traditional country breakfast and it was disagreeing with him; for yet another, he had been hauled out on yet another of his mother-in-law's picnics; finally, there was the picnic basket. The picnic basket was a family
(20) piece, dating, as Mrs. Leslie said on its every appearance, from an age of footmen. It was the size of a cabin trunk, built for eternity out of red wicker, equipped with massy cutlery and crockery; time had sharpened its red fangs,
(25) and however Leo took hold if it, they lacerated him. Also it caused him embarrassment to be seen carrying this rattling, creaking monstrosity, and today he had carried it farther than usual.

From Sylvia Townsend Warner's HEALTHY LANDSCAPE WITH DORMOUSE, © 1966

2. In the excerpt, where is Leo located?

(1) in London
(2) in a large house
(3) in a large picnic basket
(4) in the countryside
(5) at a resort

3. In the excerpt, Leo states he has been forced to go on "yet another of his mother-in-law's picnics" (lines 17–18). What could you predict about Leo, based on the tone of the excerpt?

Leo will probably

(1) love the next picnic
(2) dislike the next picnic, too
(3) tell his mother-in-law to stop having picnics
(4) ask to reschedule the picnic
(5) begin to have his own picnics

4. Leo's exposure to nature has been at "very expensive pleasure resorts" (line 7). His experience at the picnic is most like which of the following examples?

(1) A person in New Jersey takes the train to watch a Broadway show.
(2) A country couple drives to town for a dance.
(3) A Chicago lawyer does not know how to saddle a horse on a trail ride.
(4) A web designer knows a surprising amount of information about sheep.
(5) A Houston banker checks her e-mail while on vacation in the mountains.

5. Each time she uses the picnic basket, Mrs. Leslie tells people that it was first used in "an age of footmen" (line 21). Based on this knowledge of her character, what could you predict about Mrs. Leslie?

She will

(1) not tell people about her family's wealth
(2) be generally modest about her accomplishments
(3) not announce an important award she has received
(4) give money to charities anonymously
(5) find excuses to brag about her family

UNIT 2

Unit 2 Review

The Unit Review is structured to resemble the GED Language Arts/Reading Test. Be sure to read each question and all possible answers very carefully before choosing your answer. To record your answers, fill in the numbered circle that corresponds to the answer you select for each question in the Unit Review.

Do not rest your pencil on the answer area while considering your answer. Make no stray or unnecessary marks. If you change an answer, erase your first mark completely. Mark only one answer space for each question; multiple answers will be scored as incorrect.

Sample Question

For what does the speaker wish?

   (1) to meet a woman named Cleopatra
   (2) to read a new book
   (3) to travel to London
   (4) to leave Vera Cruz
   (5) to buy a drink at the bar

   ①②③●⑤

<u>Questions 1 through 6</u> refer to the following excerpt.

WHAT TYPE OF VACATION DOES THE SPEAKER WANT TO TAKE?

I could not remember when last I had had a moment to myself. I had often amused my fancy with the prospect of just one week's complete idleness. Most of us when not busy
(5) working are busy playing; we ride, play tennis or golf, swim or gamble; but I saw myself doing nothing at all. I would lounge through the morning, dawdle through the afternoon and loaf through the evening. My mind would
(10) be a slate [chalkboard] and each passing hour a sponge that wiped out the scribblings written on it by the world of sense. Time, because it is so fleeting, time, because it is beyond recall, is the most precious of human
(15) goods and to squander it is the most delicate form of dissipation in which man can indulge. Cleopatra dissolved in wine a priceless pearl, but she gave it to Antony to drink; when you waste the brief golden hours you
(20) take the beaker in which the gem is melted and dash its contents to the ground. The gesture is grand and like all grand gestures absurd. That of course is its excuse. In the week I promised myself I should naturally
(25) read, for to the habitual reader reading is a drug of which he is the slave; deprive him of printed matter and he grows nervous, moody and restless; then, like the alcoholic bereft of brandy who will drink shellac or
(30) methylated spirit, he will make do with the advertisements of a paper five years old; he will make do with a telephone directory....

But I had always fancied myself choosing my moment with surroundings to my liking,
(35) not having it forced upon me; and when I was suddenly faced with nothing to do and had to make the best of it (like a steamship acquaintance whom in the wide waste of the Pacific Ocean you have invited to stay
(40) with you in London and who turns up without warning and with all his luggage) I was not a little taken aback. I had come to Vera Cruz from Mexico City to catch one of the Ward Company's white cool ships to Yucatan; and
(45) found to my dismay that, a dock strike having been declared over-night, my ship would not put in. I was stuck in Vera Cruz.

From W. Somerset Maugham's THE BUM, © 1929

UNIT 2

1. What is the speaker's situation?

   He is

   (1) lost
   (2) sick
   (3) stranded
   (4) homesick
   (5) peaceful

   ①②③④⑤

2. Why does the speaker want to do nothing?

   The speaker has

   (1) never been to Vera Cruz
   (2) never been to Yucatan
   (3) grown bored with reading
   (4) not had time to himself
   (5) been reading too much

   ①②③④⑤

3. The speaker says that "my mind would be a slate and each passing hour a sponge" (lines 9–10). How do these metaphors play a role in this excerpt?

   (1) They describe the speaker's restless feeling.
   (2) They explain how the speaker recovers from vacation.
   (3) They are metaphors for the speaker's desire to forget things.
   (4) They symbolize the speaker's profession.
   (5) They represent the speaker's dissatisfaction with Vera Cruz.

   ①②③④⑤

4. Which word best describes the speaker's tone?

   (1) wishful
   (2) thankful
   (3) annoyed
   (4) angry
   (5) somber

   ①②③④⑤

5. In the excerpt, the speaker says that Cleopatra dissolved a "priceless pearl" in wine (lines 17–18). Based on this excerpt, why might Cleopatra have done this?

   Cleopatra wanted to

   (1) destroy an object of beauty
   (2) show her love for Antony
   (3) impoverish herself
   (4) show the quality of the wine
   (5) create a delicious drink

   ①②③④⑤

6. The feeling expressed by the speaker in the last paragraph is most like which of the following people?

   (1) a movie-goer who sits down to a fine show
   (2) a diner whose meals is brought to his table
   (3) a person receiving a package at her doorstep
   (4) a commuter hopping on the last train
   (5) a customer told that a store is out of the product she wants

   ①②③④⑤

WHICH OF THE SISTERS IS RICH, AND WHICH IS POOR?

Over the years Lottie had urged Bess to prepare for her old age. Over the years Bess had lived each day as if there were no other. Now they were both past sixty, the time for
(5) summing up. Lottie had a bank account that had never grown lean. Bess had the clothes on her back, and the rest of her worldly possession in a battered suitcase.

Lottie had hated being a child, hearing
(10) her parents' skimping and scraping. Bess had never seemed to notice. All she ever wanted was to go outside and play. She learned to skate on borrowed skates. She rode a borrowed bicycle. Lottie couldn't
(15) wait to grow up and buy herself the best of everything.

As soon as anyone would hire her, Lottie put herself to work. She minded babies, she ran errands for the old.
(20) She never touched a penny of her money, though her child's mouth watered for ice cream and candy. But she could not bear to share with Bess, who never had anything to share with her. When the dimes began
(25) to add up to dollars, she lost her taste for sweets.

By the time she was twelve, she was clerking after school in a small variety store. Saturdays she worked as long as she was
(30) wanted. She decided to keep her money for clothes. When she entered high school, she would wear a wardrobe that neither she nor anyone else would be able to match.

But her freshman year found her unable
(35) to indulge in so frivolous a whim, particularly when her admiring instructors advised her to think seriously of college. No one in her family had ever gone to college, and certainly Bess would never get there. She would show
(40) them all what she could do, if she put her mind to it.

She began to bank her money, and her bank became her most private and precious possession.
(45) In her third year high she found a job in a small but expanding restaurant, where she cashiered from the busy hour until closing. In her last year high the business increased so rapidly that Lottie was faced with the choice
(50) of staying in school or working full-time.

She made her choice easily. A job in hand was worth two in the future.

Bess had a beau in the school band, who had no other ambition except to play a horn.
(55) Lottie expected to be settled with a home and family while Bess was still waiting for Harry to earn enough to buy a marriage license.

That Bess married Harry straight out of high school was not surprising. That Lottie
(60) never married at all was not really surprising either.

From Dorothy West's THE RICHER, THE POORER, © 1967

7. At age 60, the sisters reach "the time for summing up" (lines 4–5). What information about Lottie and Bess is being analyzed?

   (1) the number of their children
   (2) the money they have in the bank
   (3) the dresses in their closets
   (4) what they have done with their lives
   (5) what they learned in school

   ①②③④⑤

8. Based on the information about Lottie's character, what might she do if offered a satisfying job that paid very little money?

   Lottie would probably

   (1) take the job immediately
   (2) agonize over whether to take the job
   (3) tell Bess about the job
   (4) sadly decline the job
   (5) never consider taking the job

   ①②③④⑤

9. What might be the author's purpose in describing the two sisters?

   (1) to compare their approaches to education
   (2) to contrast their attitudes about money
   (3) to illustrate the difficulty of marrying young
   (4) to show the importance of preparation
   (5) to examine the sisters' greed

   ①②③④⑤

10. Which word describes Lottie's life?

    (1) difficult
    (2) invigorating
    (3) placid
    (4) exciting
    (5) secure

    ①②③④⑤

11. Bess is the type of person who "lived each day as if there were no other" (line 3). Which of the following examples most resembles Bess?

    Bess is most like a person who

    (1) attends church services every day
    (2) borrows sugar from her neighbors to bake cookies
    (3) charges items to credit cards but does not pay for them
    (4) fills up on appetizers instead of waiting for a meal
    (5) makes fruit preserves for the winter

    ①②③④⑤

12. What can you infer about Lottie from the statement that Lottie "never touched a penny of her money, though her child's mouth watered for ice cream and candy" (lines 20–22)?

    (1) She has no children.
    (2) She did not spend money on unnecessary items.
    (3) She made her children earn their own money.
    (4) She hated ice cream and candy.
    (5) She thought food was too expensive.

    ①②③④⑤

Unit 3

JIMMY SANTIAGO BACA

Jimmy Santiago Baca overcame adversity to turn his life around and earn his GED certificate.

It was only after Jimmy Santiago Baca left society that he decided to improve it. As a teenager, Baca ran away from an orphanage, lived on the streets of New Mexico, and was arrested and convicted of drug possession. The conviction brought with it a five-year prison sentence, most of them spent in isolation.

In prison, Baca turned his life around. He learned to read and write and even discovered a passion for poetry. In 1979, the same year in which he was released from prison, three of Baca's poems were published by a national magazine. That same year, Baca studied for and received his GED certificate.

Baca furthered his education by earning a bachelor's degree in English and receiving a Ph.D. in literature. Since then, he has written poems, novels, and film scripts. His past is a prominent theme in his writing. He often writes about American Southwest barrios, or Spanish-speaking neighborhoods like those in which he lived in as a child. Baca's themes also include addiction, injustice, and education. He believes poetry describes experiences common to everyone. As he notes,

> **❝ Poetry transcends all colors and cultures, and ultimately beats from the red heart. ❞**

Baca has committed to helping others who face challenges in life. He created Cedar Tree, Inc., a nonprofit foundation that provides free writing instruction, books, and materials. The organization also offers scholarships. Baca also holds writing workshops in prisons, libraries, and community centers around the country. He feels literature changed his life and that it can change the lives of others.

BIO BLAST: Jimmy Santiago Baca

- Raised by his grandmother and in an orphanage before running away at age 13
- Received his undergraduate degree in English and an honorary doctorate in literature from the University of New Mexico

- Earned numerous national and international awards for his writing
- Founded Cedar Tree, Inc., to help people become educated and improve their lives
- Received the Cornelius P. Turner award, which is given each year to an outstanding GED graduate

Unit 3: Poetry

Poetry is a special kind of writing that appeals to people's emotions and senses through the use of descriptive language. Poets such as Jimmy Santiago Baca write poems to express their feelings or even to tell stories. You can read poems in books, magazines, or on the Internet. You also can hear a type of poetry—song lyrics—when you listen to music.

On the GED Language Arts/Reading Test, poetry makes up a part of the overall literature passages. Unlike fiction texts, which are written in sentences and paragraphs, poetry is often written in lines or groups of lines called stanzas. In Unit 3, the introduction of ideas such as rhythm and rhyme, analogies, and restatement will help you prepare for the GED Language Arts/Reading Test.

Table of Contents

Rhythm and Rhyme

① Learn the Skill

Rhythm and **rhyme** are sound effects that influence a reader's understanding of poetry. Rhythm is a pattern of stressed syllables. In the phrase "'Twas the night before Christmas," for example, every third syllable is stressed—"'Twas the *night* before *Christ*mas." Rhythm can be created by the use of punctuation and line breaks. Words that rhyme may have similar vowel or consonant sounds, such as *teach* and *peach*. **Partial rhymes**, such as *teach* and *team*, include words that do not rhyme completely. To determine a rhyming pattern, assign a letter to the last word (the rhyming word) of a line of a stanza, as shown below. A **stanza** is a section of a poem, similar to a paragraph of fiction.

② Practice the Skill

By mastering the skill of identifying a poem's rhythm and rhyme, you will improve your study and test-taking skills, especially as they relate to the GED Language Arts/Reading Test. Read the excerpt and strategies below. Then answer the question that follows.

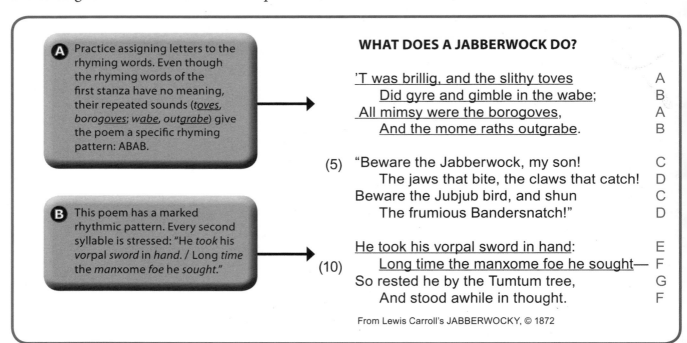

Ⓐ Practice assigning letters to the rhyming words. Even though the rhyming words of the first stanza have no meaning, their repeated sounds (*toves*, *borogoves*; *wabe*, *outgrabe*) give the poem a specific rhyming pattern: ABAB.

Ⓑ This poem has a marked rhythmic pattern. Every second syllable is stressed: "He *took* his *vorpal sword* in *hand*. / Long *time* the *man*xome *foe* he *sought*."

WHAT DOES A JABBERWOCK DO?

'T was brillig, and the slithy toves	A
Did gyre and gimble in the wabe;	B
All mimsy were the borogoves,	A
And the mome raths outgrabe.	B
(5) "Beware the Jabberwock, my son!	C
The jaws that bite, the claws that catch!	D
Beware the Jubjub bird, and shun	C
The frumious Bandersnatch!"	D
He took his vorpal sword in hand:	E
(10) Long time the manxome foe he sought—	F
So rested he by the Tumtum tree,	G
And stood awhile in thought.	F

From Lewis Carroll's JABBERWOCKY, © 1872

✓ TEST-TAKING TIPS

Many poems were written to be read aloud. Softly saying a poem aloud can give you an idea of its rhythm and where the stressed syllables are.

1. How would you describe the rhythm in this poem?

   (1) surprising and offbeat
   (2) delicate and graceful
   (3) regular and reliable
   (4) lurching and unsteady
   (5) heavy and oppressive

Directions: Choose the <u>one best answer</u> to each question.

Questions 2 and 3 refer to the following poem.

WHAT MAKES THIS DESCRIPTION UNUSUAL?

The Panther

The panther is like a leopard,
Except it hasn't been peppered.
Should you behold a panther crouch,
Prepare to say Ouch.
(5) Better yet, if called by a panther,
Don't anther.

Ogden Nash's THE PANTHER, © 1940

2. What is the effect of the rhyme in the poem's last two lines (lines 5–6)?

   Readers are probably

   (1) amused by the rhyme of "panther" and "anther"
   (2) upset that "anther" is not a real word
   (3) unsure how to pronounce "anther"
   (4) confused because answer is not spelled correctly
   (5) annoyed because "panther" does not rhyme with "anther"

3. "Don't anther" (line 6) is much shorter than the poem's other lines. What was the author's purpose in creating this type of rhythm?

   The author probably wanted to

   (1) create a regular rhythm
   (2) make the rhythm like a graceful panther
   (3) emphasize that the poem ends abruptly
   (4) show how a rhythm can be soothing
   (5) build a sense of movement

Questions 4 and 5 refer to the following poem.

WHAT GIFT DOES THE SPEAKER WANT?

One Perfect Rose

A single flow'r he sent me, since we met.
All tenderly his messenger he chose;
Deep-hearted, pure, with scented dew still wet—
(5) One perfect rose.

I knew the language of the floweret;
"My fragile leaves," it said, "his heart enclose."
Love long has taken for his amulet
(10) One perfect rose.

Why is it no one has ever sent me yet
One perfect limousine, do you suppose?
Ah no, it's always just my luck to get
One perfect rose.

Dorothy Parker's ONE PERFECT ROSE, © 1926

4. Which best describes the poem's rhythm?

   (1) bouncy
   (2) jerky
   (3) formal
   (4) pounding
   (5) upbeat

5. Which of the following items would the speaker probably choose for a present?

   (1) a sentimental key chain
   (2) an inexpensive piece of costume jewelry
   (3) a puppy from an animal shelter
   (4) a jewelry store gift certificate
   (5) an antique handkerchief

Analogies

① Learn the Skill

Poets often use **analogies** in their poems to compare two things to highlight similarities and differences. You learned about some forms of analogies in Unit 2. Analogies may take the form of **metaphors**, which describe one thing as being another: *My love is a rose*. **Similes** are another type of analogy that make comparisons by using the words *like* or *as*: *My street is as crooked as a maze* or *My love is like a rose*. Poets use similes and metaphors to make unusual comparisons that create memorable images.

② Practice the Skill

By mastering the skill of analyzing analogies, you will improve your study and test-taking skills, especially as they relate to the GED Language Arts/Reading Test. Read the poem and strategies below. Then answer the question that follows.

Ⓐ In this analogy, the speaker compares a book to a frigate, which is a type of ship. This comparison uses the word *like*, which means it is a simile.

Ⓑ The speaker says that a chariot carries away the human soul. Here, a chariot is a metaphor for the book that carries the speaker to far-away lands.

HOW CAN THE SPEAKER GO SO MANY PLACES?

There Is No Frigate Like a Book

Ⓐ There is no frigate [ship] like a book
   To take us lands away,
Nor any coursers [horses] like a page
   Of prancing poetry.

(5) This traverse [travel] may the poorest take
   Without oppress of toll;
Ⓑ How frugal is the chariot
   That bears a human soul!

Emily Dickinson's THERE IS NO FRIGATE LIKE A BOOK, © 1924

USING LOGIC

To analyze analogies, look for extended comparisons that may carry through the entire poem. Here the speaker compares books to different types of transportation that can carry her mind far away, even while her body remains in the same place.

1. In what way is a book similar to a sailing ship?

   It is

   (1) available to people with little money
   (2) only found at the library
   (3) sold at the seaside
   (4) able to take readers to distant places
   (5) large and expensive

Directions: Choose the <u>one best answer</u> to each question.

<u>Questions 2 through 5</u> refer to the following poem.

HOW DO OLD FRIENDS FEEL ABOUT SEEING ONE ANOTHER?

The Meeting

After so long an absence
    At last we meet again:
Does the meeting give us pleasure,
    Or does it give us pain?

(5) The tree of life has been shaken,
    And but few of us linger now,
Like the Prophet's two or three berries
    In the top of the uppermost bough.

We cordially greet each other
(10)   In the old, familiar tone;
And we think, though we do not say it,
    How old and gray he is grown!

We speak of a Merry Christmas
    And many a Happy New Year;
(15) But each in his heart is thinking
    Of those that are not here.

We speak of friends and their fortunes,
    And what they did and said,
Till the dead alone seem living
(20)   And the living alone seem dead.

At last we hardly distinguish
    Between the ghosts and the guests;
And a mist and shadow of sadness
    Steals over our merriest jests.

Henry Wadsworth Longfellow's THE MEETING

2. What saddens the speaker about meeting his old friend?

   (1) They have nothing in common.
   (2) They will not have a Merry Christmas.
   (3) Many of their friends have died.
   (4) They are no longer friendly.
   (5) Their fortunes have been lost.

3. The speaker says that the friends are "Like the Prophet's two or three berries" in the top of a tree (line 7–8). What does this comparison reveal about the friends?

   The friends are

   (1) special, like delicious fruit on a tree
   (2) hard to reach
   (3) part of a prophecy
   (4) like trees in a forest
   (5) among a very few who still remain

4. Which word identifies the feeling of the poem?

   (1) angry
   (2) disappointed
   (3) wistful
   (4) fearful
   (5) joyous

5. The feelings expressed by the speaker in the last stanza (lines 21–24) are most like which of the following people?

   (1) a person trying, but failing, to enjoy her birthday party
   (2) a host welcoming guests to a party
   (3) a child failing to blow out the candles on a cake
   (4) a helper distributing gift bags as guests leave
   (5) a guest eating snacks at a Christmas party

UNIT 3

Figurative Language

1 Learn the Skill

As you learned in Unit 2, **figurative language** is the use of symbols, phrases, and ideas that give words a meaning beyond their ordinary meaning. Examples of figurative language may include **personification**, in which non-living objects are given human or animal qualities. For example: *The dirty dishes looked sullenly from the sink*. **Exaggeration**, also called **hyperbole**, is a type of figurative language used for emphasis or humor. *I told you a million times* is an example of exaggeration.

2 Practice the Skill

By being able to identify the figurative language in a literary work, you will improve your study and test-taking skills, especially as they relate to the GED Language Arts/Reading Test. Read the excerpt and strategies below. Then answer the questions that follow.

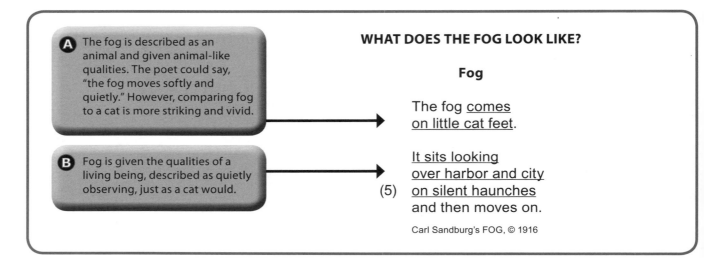

A The fog is described as an animal and given animal-like qualities. The poet could say, "the fog moves softly and quietly." However, comparing fog to a cat is more striking and vivid.

B Fog is given the qualities of a living being, described as quietly observing, just as a cat would.

WHAT DOES THE FOG LOOK LIKE?

Fog

The fog <u>comes
on little cat feet</u>.

<u>It sits looking
over harbor and city</u>
(5) <u>on silent haunches</u>
and then moves on.

Carl Sandburg's FOG, © 1916

☑ TEST-TAKING TIPS

When reading for personification, think about what similarities the poet would want a reader to see in the comparison he or she is making. In "Fog," for example, the poet asks readers to think about how a cat moves: smoothly, quickly, silently.

1. The fog is described as having "cat feet" (line 2). What can we tell about fog from this description?

   (1) It is furry.
   (2) It is quiet.
   (3) It has whiskers.
   (4) It purrs loudly.
   (5) It scratches fiercely.

2. Why might the poet have used personification?

   (1) The fog looked human that day.
   (2) It reminded him of a friend.
   (3) It helps the reader identify with the fog.
   (4) He wanted the fog to seem ominous.
   (5) The fog appeared to take human form.

Directions: Choose the <u>one best answer</u> to each question.

<u>Questions 3 through 6</u> refer to the following poem.

HOW MUCH TIME DOES THE SPEAKER HAVE TO LOVE HIS LADY?

To His Coy Mistress

Had we but world enough, and time,
This coyness, Lady, were no crime
We would sit down and think which way
To walk and pass our long love's day.
(5) Thou by the Indian Ganges' [a river] side
Shouldst rubies find: I by the tide
Of Humber [a river] would complain. I would
Love you ten years before the Flood,
And you should, if you please, refuse
(10) Till the conversion of the Jews.
My vegetable love should grow
Vaster than empires, and more slow;
An hundred years should go to praise
Thine eyes and on thy forehead gaze;
(15) Two hundred to adore each breast,
But thirty thousand to the rest;
An age at least to every part,
And the last age should show your heart.
For, Lady, you deserve this state,
(20) Nor would I love at lower rate.
    But at my back I always hear
Time's wingèd chariot hurrying near;
And yonder all before us lie
Deserts of vast eternity.

From Andrew Marvell's TO HIS COY MISTRESS, © 1919

3. What does the speaker claim he would do if time permitted?

He would

(1) love his mistress for hundreds of years
(2) stop loving his mistress
(3) visit the Ganges River
(4) prevent a flood
(5) ride for miles on time's chariot

4. Time is a recurring theme in this poem. What does the speaker's description of time suggest?

(1) He does not have time for a relationship.
(2) His mistress is running out of time.
(3) He is exaggerating time for effect.
(4) He knows that love is timeless.
(5) He resists hurrying because he likes taking his time.

5. The speaker states that his love will grow "Vaster than empires" (line 11–12). Which of the following examples most resembles this statement?

(1) Rome wasn't built in a day.
(2) All's fair in love and war.
(3) A penny saved is a penny earned.
(4) Waste not, want not.
(5) I'll give you the moon.

6. The speaker says, "But at my back I always hear / Time's wingèd chariot hurrying near" (lines 21–22). What can you infer about the speaker?

He knows that

(1) time travels on wings
(2) he has all the time in the world
(3) time continues to pass
(4) his mistress has a deadline
(5) he has to stop time

Symbols and Imagery

1 Learn the Skill

As you learned in Unit 2, people recognize many symbols in daily life. A flag, for example, symbolizes a country, while a mascot can symbolize a sports team. Poets use **symbols** to stand for important ideas and concepts. A huge tree, for example, might symbolize a family's home and heritage. **Imagery** in poetry describes the taste, touch, smell, sound, and appearance of objects to make them vivid to the reader.

2 Practice the Skill

By mastering the skill of identifying symbols and images, you will improve your study and test-taking skills, especially as they relate to the GED Language Arts/Reading Test. Read the excerpt and strategies below. Then answer the question that follows.

A The speaker describes the smell of whiskey on his father's breath. This sensory detail adds to the imagery of the boy and his father.

B The speaker includes details about the father's hands. How does the image of the father's hands affect your reading of the poem?

HOW WELL DOES THIS FATHER DANCE?

My Papa's Waltz

A The whiskey on your breath
Could make a small boy dizzy;
But I hung on like death:
Such waltzing was not easy.

(5) We romped until the pans
Slid from the kitchen shelf;
My mother's countenance
Could not unfrown itself.

The hand that held my wrist
(10) Was battered on one knuckle;
At every step you missed
B My right ear scraped a buckle.

You beat time on my head
With a palm caked hard by dirt,
(15) Then waltzed me off to bed
Still clinging to your shirt.

Theodore Roethke's MY PAPA'S WALTZ, © 1942

✓ **TEST-TAKING TIPS**

To find examples of imagery, look for examples that help you feel as if you are part of the poem. If the poem includes details that help you imagine particular sights, smells, sounds, feelings, or tastes, then those details are examples of imagery.

1. The poem describes the father's hands as "battered on one knuckle" (line 10). How does this imagery add to the poem?

   It shows that the father

   (1) has been in a fight
   (2) is careless
   (3) works in an office
   (4) is vain about his appearance
   (5) never works outside

UNIT 3

Directions: Choose the <u>one best answer</u> to each question.

<u>Questions 2 through 6</u> refer to the following poem.

WHERE DOES THIS ROAD LEAD?

Uphill

Does the road wind uphill all the way?
    Yes, to the very end.
Will the day's journey take the whole long day?
    From morn to night, my friend.

(5) But is there for the night a resting-place?
    A roof for when the slow, dark hours begin.
May not the darkness hide it from my face?
    You cannot miss that inn.

Shall I meet other wayfarers at night?
(10)   Those who have gone before.
Then must I knock, or call when just in sight?
    They will not keep you waiting at that door.

Shall I find comfort, travel-sore and weak?
    Of labour you shall find the sum.
(15) Will there be beds for me and all who seek?
    Yea, beds for all who come.

Christina Rossetti's UPHILL, © 1862

2. What conversation takes place in the first stanza (lines 1–4)?

A traveler

(1) asks about a journey
(2) gets supplies for a trip
(3) asks for directions
(4) makes reservations
(5) pays for a vacation

3. The first speaker predicts the journey will leave travelers "travel-sore and weak" (line 13). What does this tell us about the trip?

(1) It will be easy.
(2) It will be downhill.
(3) It will be long.
(4) It will be on horseback.
(5) It will be by automobile.

4. Based on the details in the poem, what might the road symbolize?

The road is a symbol for

(1) hope
(2) peace
(3) failure
(4) life
(5) love

5. The second speaker states that there will be "beds for all who come" (line 16). Which of the following statements is most like this statement?

(1) Please knock before you enter.
(2) The door is always open to you.
(3) Do not disturb.
(4) Checkout time is at noon.
(5) The key is under the welcome mat.

6. In the poem, a second speaker answers questions with replies such as "They will not keep you waiting at that door" (line 12). Which word best describes the tone of these replies?

(1) alarming
(2) threatening
(3) foreboding
(4) disappointing
(5) comforting

Make Inferences

① Learn the Skill

Readers **make inferences** when they make educated guesses about meanings that are unclear or incomplete. To make inferences, readers combine what they know about a topic with the evidence found in the poem. In addition, readers can use what they know about symbols and images, as discussed in Lesson 4, to help determine what ideas the poet has suggested or otherwise implied.

② Practice the Skill

By mastering the skill of making inferences, you will improve your study and test-taking skills, especially as they relate to the GED Language Arts/Reading Test. Read the excerpt and strategies below. Then answer the question that follows.

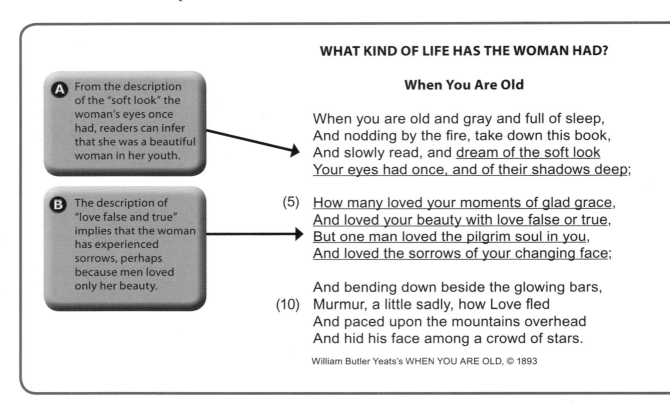

WHAT KIND OF LIFE HAS THE WOMAN HAD?

When You Are Old

When you are old and gray and full of sleep,
And nodding by the fire, take down this book,
And slowly read, and dream of the soft look
Your eyes had once, and of their shadows deep;

(5)   How many loved your moments of glad grace,
And loved your beauty with love false or true,
But one man loved the pilgrim soul in you,
And loved the sorrows of your changing face;

And bending down beside the glowing bars,
(10)   Murmur, a little sadly, how Love fled
And paced upon the mountains overhead
And hid his face among a crowd of stars.

William Butler Yeats's WHEN YOU ARE OLD, © 1893

A From the description of the "soft look" the woman's eyes once had, readers can infer that she was a beautiful woman in her youth.

B The description of "love false and true" implies that the woman has experienced sorrows, perhaps because men loved only her beauty.

USING LOGIC

By examining the compassionate description of the woman, readers could infer that the speaker himself is the "one man" who loved the woman truly.

1. What can you infer about the woman based on her behavior?

    (1) No man ever loved her.
    (2) Her love has died.
    (3) She is pleased to have had many suitors.
    (4) She is sad that she was never beautiful.
    (5) She was never disappointed by love.

Directions: Choose the one best answer to each question.

Questions 2 through 6 refer to the following poem.

WHY IS THE MAN LOOKING AT THE FLOWER?

The Woodspurge

The wind flapp'd loose, the wind was still,
Shaken out dead from tree and hill:
I had walk'd on at the wind's will,—
I sat now, for the wind was still.

(5) Between my knees my forehead was,—
My lips, drawn in, said not Alas!
My hair was over in the grass,
My naked ears heard the day pass.

My eyes, wide open, had the run
(10) Of some ten weeds to fix upon;
Among those few, out of the sun,
The woodspurge flower'd, three cups in one.

From perfect grief there need not be
Wisdom or even memory:
(15) One thing then learnt remains to me,—
The woodspurge has a cup of three.

Dante Gabriel Rossetti's THE WOODSPURGE, © 1856

2. From the evidence in the poem, what can we infer about this man?

(1) He is grieving.
(2) He is studying flowers.
(3) He loves nature.
(4) He is monitoring the weather.
(5) He values wisdom.

3. What is the man's position in lines 5 through 8?

He is

(1) walking up a hill
(2) sitting with his hands between his knees
(3) sitting with his head between his knees
(4) standing with his feet in the grass
(5) sitting with his eyes closed

4. The speaker examines the flowers and states, "The woodspurge has a cup of three" (line 16). What might this observation mean?

From the speaker's behavior, we can infer that this information

(1) is important to him
(2) is all he can think about in his grief
(3) gives him wisdom he can share with others
(4) reminds him of something
(5) gives him comfort

5. What is the tone of the poem?

(1) confused
(2) forgiving
(3) indifferent
(4) desolate
(5) combative

6. What does the first stanza tell us about the speaker?

(1) He was dead until the wind shook him.
(2) He's in the middle of a storm.
(3) He is sitting in a tree on the top of a hill.
(4) His jacket flaps in the wind.
(5) His movements have been dictated by the wind.

Restatement

① Learn the Skill

Identifying a poem's main idea can help you better understand and analyze what the poet is saying. One strategy to help identify a poem's main idea is **restatement**. Restating the poet's ideas in your own words can help you unlock the meanings of poems and identify a poem's most important message.

② Practice the Skill

By mastering the skill of restatement, you will improve your study and test-taking skills, especially as they relate to the GED Language Arts/Reading Test. Read the excerpt and strategies below. Then answer the question that follows.

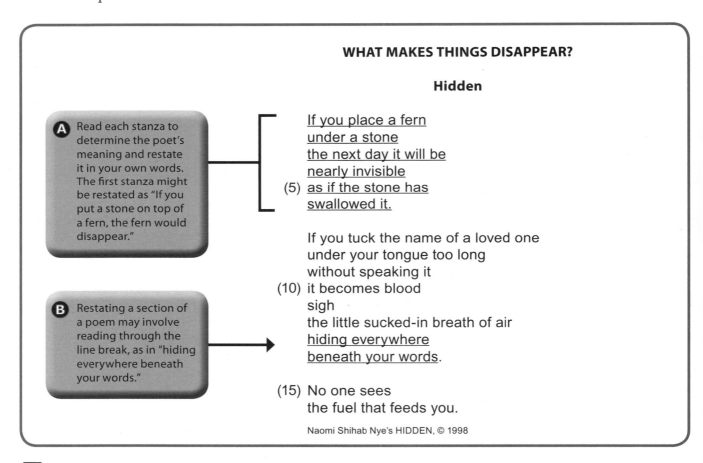

WHAT MAKES THINGS DISAPPEAR?

Hidden

A Read each stanza to determine the poet's meaning and restate it in your own words. The first stanza might be restated as "If you put a stone on top of a fern, the fern would disappear."

If you place a fern
under a stone
the next day it will be
nearly invisible
(5) as if the stone has
swallowed it.

If you tuck the name of a loved one
under your tongue too long
without speaking it
(10) it becomes blood
sigh
the little sucked-in breath of air
hiding everywhere
beneath your words.

B Restating a section of a poem may involve reading through the line break, as in "hiding everywhere beneath your words."

(15) No one sees
the fuel that feeds you.

Naomi Shihab Nye's HIDDEN, © 1998

MAKING ASSUMPTIONS

When restating a poem, you may assume that many images are not describing a literal action.

1. What is one way of restating lines 15 and 16?

    (1) The people we love give us invisible strength.
    (2) We should not talk about loved ones.
    (3) People need fuel, just like machines.
    (4) We should not reveal the source of our fuel.
    (5) We should make sure that everyone has enough to eat.

Directions: Choose the <u>one best answer</u> to each question.

<u>Questions 2 through 6</u> refer to the following poem.

WHAT DOES THE NEW YEAR BRING?

I Stood on a Tower

I stood on a tower in the wet,
And New Year and the Old Year met,
And winds were roaring and blowing;
And I said, "O years that meet in tears,
(5) Have ye aught that is worth the knowing?

"Science enough and exploring
Wanderers coming and going
Matter enough for deploring
But aught that is worth the knowing?"

(10) Seas at my feet were flowing
Waves on the shingle pouring,
Old Year roaring and blowing
And New Year blowing and roaring.

Alfred Lord Tennyson's I STOOD ON A TOWER, © 1868

2. What does the speaker mean by saying the "New Year and the Old Year met" (line 2)?

The speaker

(1) has been on the tower for a year
(2) wants the New Year to come
(3) is on the tower on New Year's Eve
(4) wants to celebrate the New Year
(5) is grieving for the Old Year

3. What does the speaker imply by his description of "years that meet in tears" (line 4)?

(1) The time is joyous.
(2) It is a difficult time.
(3) It has stopped raining.
(4) Rain resembles tears.
(5) The New Year will be better than the Old.

4. Which of the following is the best restatement of the second stanza (lines 6–9)?

(1) Which explorations should we know about?
(2) How can we gather more scientific information?
(3) How much of our new information is useful?
(4) Why is so much information useless?
(5) How can we ignore the unimportant information?

5. The feelings expressed by the speaker in the second stanza (lines 6–9) are most like which of the following people?

(1) an engineer programming a new computer
(2) a teenager text-messaging a friend
(3) a teacher answering an instant-message question
(4) a parent coping with rapidly changing technology
(5) a librarian monitoring patrons' Internet use

6. Which word identifies the tone of the poem?

(1) complacent
(2) uneasy
(3) confident
(4) romantic
(5) grateful

UNIT 3

Theme

① Learn the Skill

In Lesson 5, you practiced how to make inferences about meanings that were suggested but not explicitly stated in a poem. Making inferences is important when looking for the **theme**, or main idea, of a poem. A poem's theme reveals something about human nature, such as a lesson about life. Use what you know to make inferences about images, symbols, and figurative language; these inferences will help you identify the poet's opinions or beliefs on a larger topic.

② Practice the Skill

By mastering the skill of identifying a poem's theme, you will improve your study and test-taking skills, especially as they relate to the GED Language Arts/Reading Test. Read the excerpt and strategies below. Then answer the question that follows.

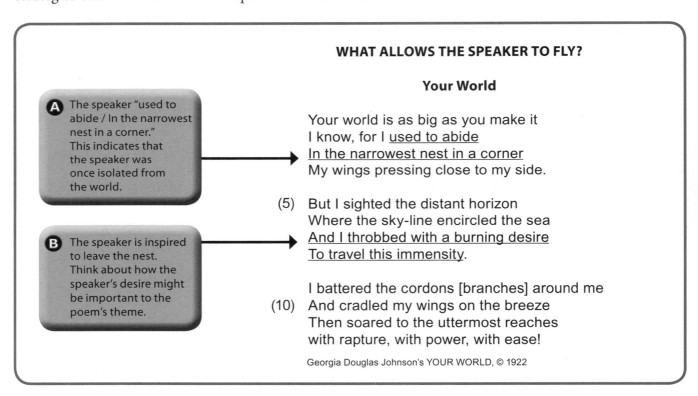

WHAT ALLOWS THE SPEAKER TO FLY?

Your World

A The speaker "used to abide / In the narrowest nest in a corner." This indicates that the speaker was once isolated from the world.

B The speaker is inspired to leave the nest. Think about how the speaker's desire might be important to the poem's theme.

Your world is as big as you make it
I know, for I <u>used to abide</u>
<u>In the narrowest nest in a corner</u>
My wings pressing close to my side.

(5) But I sighted the distant horizon
Where the sky-line encircled the sea
<u>And I throbbed with a burning desire</u>
<u>To travel this immensity</u>.

I battered the cordons [branches] around me
(10) And cradled my wings on the breeze
Then soared to the uttermost reaches
with rapture, with power, with ease!

Georgia Douglas Johnson's YOUR WORLD, © 1922

☑ TEST-TAKING TIPS

Remember that themes teach a larger lesson about ourselves or about humanity. The subject of this poem is flying through the world, but the theme of the poem shares a larger ideal.

1. Which of the following best describes the theme of the poem?

(1) Birds enjoy the sensation of flight.
(2) All birds like to fly along the shore.
(3) People should stick to the places they know.
(4) The world is not as big as we think it is.
(5) A person can go anywhere and do anything if he or she only tries to do it.

Directions: Choose the <u>one best answer</u> to each question.

Questions 2 through 5 refer to the following:

WHAT EVENT IS THE SPEAKER DESCRIBING?

The Second Coming

Turning and turning in the widening gyre [spiral]
The falcon cannot hear the falconer;
Things fall apart; the centre cannot hold;
Mere anarchy is loosed upon the world,
(5)   The blood-dimmed tide is loosed, and everywhere
The ceremony of innocence is drowned;
The best lack all conviction, while the worst
Are full of passionate intensity.

(10) Surely some revelation is at hand;
Surely the Second Coming is at hand.
The Second Coming! Hardly are those words out
When a vast image out of Spiritus Mundi
(15) Troubles my sight: somewhere in sands of the desert
A shape with lion body and the head of a man,
A gaze blank and pitiless as the sun,
Is moving its slow thighs, while all about it
(20) Reel shadows of the indignant desert birds.
The darkness drops again; but now I know
That twenty centuries of stony sleep
Were vexed to the nightmare by a rocking cradle,
(25) And what rough beast, its hour come round at last,
Slouches towards Bethlehem to be born?

William Butler Yeats' THE SECOND COMING, 1921

2. What does the speaker mean when he says "The falcon cannot hear the falconer; / Things fall apart; the centre cannot hold" (lines 2–3)?

The speaker

(1) believes the falcon is holding onto the center of a ball
(2) believes that events in the world are out of control
(3) has taken up falconry, but is not very good at controlling the bird
(4) thinks birds should not fly in circles
(5) understands that most birds are deaf

3. What word best describes the tone of the poem?

(1) hopeful
(2) blank
(3) worried
(4) untroubled
(5) sarcastic

4. This poem was written at the end of World War I as a protest against the political events of the time, such as the war and the Russian Revolution. Based on this information, what might the speaker be implying when he says, "The best lack all conviction, while the worst / Are full of passionate intensity" (lines 8–9)?

(1) People with worse intentions are those who speak the loudest.
(2) All the great thinkers are convicted of crimes.
(3) The worst falcons fly with the most passion.
(4) People are neither good nor bad, though some are more intense than others.
(5) People who are perceived as good are actually lacking conviction.

5. Which of the following best states the theme of this poem?

(1) Birds are omens of bad luck.
(2) The world ends not with a bang, but a whimper.
(3) Innocence is lost.
(4) The evil of men will bring about the end of the world.
(5) Everyone suffers when good men do nothing.

Unit 3 Review

The Unit Review is structured to resemble the GED Language Arts/Reading Test. Be sure to read each question and all possible answers very carefully before choosing your answer. To record your answers, fill in the numbered circle that corresponds to the answer you select for each question in the Unit Review.

Do not rest your pencil on the answer area while considering your answer. Make no stray or unnecessary marks. If you change an answer, erase your first mark completely. Mark only one answer space for each question; multiple answers will be scored as incorrect.

Sample Question

How does the poet view the setting?

(1) The poet considers the location to be dirty.
(2) The poet sees it as beautiful as he remembered.
(3) The poet wishes he was somewhere else.
(4) The poet wants winter to be over.
(5) The poet wishes more people were around.

Questions 1 through 6 refer to the following poem.

HOW CAN THE POET'S ATTITUDE BE DESCRIBED?

**Lines Composed a Few Miles Above Tintern Abbey
On Revisiting the Banks of the Wye During a Tour. July 13, 1798**

Five years have passed; five summers, with the length
Of five long winters! and again I hear
These waters, rolling from their mountain-springs
With a soft inland murmur.—Once again
(5) Do I behold these steep and lofty cliffs,
That on a wild secluded scene impress
Thoughts of more deep seclusion; and connect
The landscape with the quiet of the sky.
The day is come when I again repose
(10) Here, under this dark sycamore, and view
These plots of cottage-ground, these orchard-tufts,
Which at this season, with their unripe fruits,
Are clad in one green hue, and lose themselves
'Mid groves and copses. Once again I see
(15) These hedge-rows, hardly hedge-rows, as little lines
Of sportive wood run wild: these pastoral farms,
Green to the very door; and wreaths of smoke
Sent up, in silence, from among the trees!
With some uncertain notice, as might seem
(20) Of vagrant dwellers in the houseless woods,
Or of some Hermit's cave, where by his fire
The Hermit sits alone.

From William Wordsworth's TINTERN ABBEY

Unit 4: Drama

Drama is a type of literature that actors bring to life through performances. You have watched dramas on television, at the movies, or in theaters. Actors in dramas, such as Chris Rock, face conflict and work to resolve important issues. Dialogue helps to advance the plot and provide information about the different characters in the performance. Stage directions help you to understand a character's actions as he or she speaks. The dialogue and movements, along with scenery and music, combine to create an overall mood of the performance.

In Unit 4, you will learn to analyze drama through the careful consideration of dramatic elements such as plot, character, motivation, and mood. These skills will help you prepare for the GED Language Arts/Reading Test.

Table of Contents

Understand Plot

Drama

① *Learn the Skill*

The structure of a play is similar to that of a story. The play progresses in acts, or sections. The **plot** of a play begins with the **exposition**, which provides background information. During the course of the play, **complications** take place that lead to conflict. The **climax** is the point when the tension, caused by the rising action of the conflicts, is the greatest. After the climax, the tension of the play lessens, and problems come to an end during the **resolution**.

② *Practice the Skill*

By mastering the skill of understanding plot, you will improve your study and test-taking skills, especially as they relate to the GED Language Arts/Reading Test. Read the summary and strategies below. Then answer the question that follows.

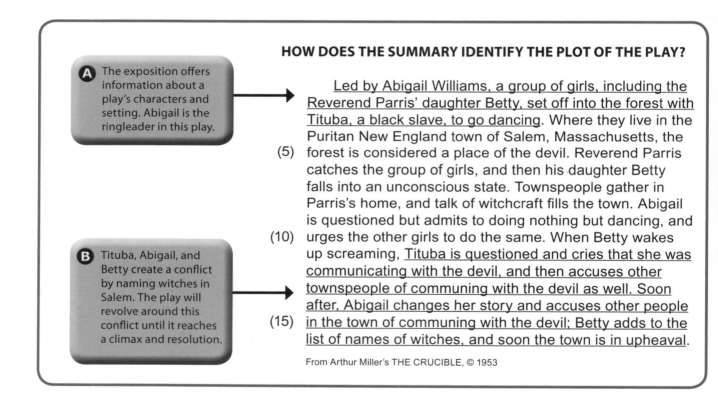

A The exposition offers information about a play's characters and setting. Abigail is the ringleader in this play.

B Tituba, Abigail, and Betty create a conflict by naming witches in Salem. The play will revolve around this conflict until it reaches a climax and resolution.

HOW DOES THE SUMMARY IDENTIFY THE PLOT OF THE PLAY?

Led by Abigail Williams, a group of girls, including the Reverend Parris' daughter Betty, set off into the forest with Tituba, a black slave, to go dancing. Where they live in the Puritan New England town of Salem, Massachusetts, the
(5) forest is considered a place of the devil. Reverend Parris catches the group of girls, and then his daughter Betty falls into an unconscious state. Townspeople gather in Parris's home, and talk of witchcraft fills the town. Abigail is questioned but admits to doing nothing but dancing, and
(10) urges the other girls to do the same. When Betty wakes up screaming, Tituba is questioned and cries that she was communicating with the devil, and then accuses other townspeople of communing with the devil as well. Soon after, Abigail changes her story and accuses other people
(15) in the town of communing with the devil; Betty adds to the list of names of witches, and soon the town is in upheaval.

From Arthur Miller's THE CRUCIBLE, © 1953

💡 USING LOGIC

Look for clues to help you determine the climax and resolution. Notice how the tension becomes greater as more women are accused.

1. Which detail is the best example of exposition?

   (1) Reverend Parris caught the girls.
   (2) Betty woke up screaming.
   (3) Abigail accused people of witchcraft.
   (4) They live in Salem, Massachusetts.
   (5) The town is in upheaval after people are named witches.

UNIT 4

Directions: Choose the <u>one best answer</u> to each question.

<u>Questions 2 through 4</u> refer to the following excerpt.

WHAT ARE THESE CHARACTERS DISCUSSING?

CHILD: Today is the day of atonement.
FAUSTUS: Of atonement…
CHILD: You bear a petition.
FAUSTUS: I do.
(5) CHILD: Say it to me.
FAUSTUS: Yes, I shall—my angel—that my
    wife, that my child, and myself may return,
    to the earth, whole, and restored, as
    before.
(10) CHILD: Whole and restored.
FAUSTUS: Bear my plea. Best of the two
    worlds. Through all my criminal confusion
    one truth endured, undoubted, and pure.
    That of your love—pity me, and preach
(15)   your benignity [compassion] in my cause
    on high.
CHILD: I shall.
FAUSTUS: Praise God—Oh, praise God.
CHILD: But to plead in the cause of whom?
(20)   *(Pause)*
FAUSTUS: Can you not know me?
CHILD: How should I know you? *(Pause)* Am I
    not endless blessed?
FAUSTUS: You are.
(25) CHILD: In what could eternal blessing consist
    save in oblivion? *(Pause)*
FAUSTUS: …my son.
CHILD: Am I your son?
FAUSTUS: Surely there's a residuary
(30)   [remaining] memory. An ineradicable
    [indestructible] memory.
CHILD: Of?
FAUSTUS: Of love. Between a father and son.
    Which transcends death. I know it. In my
(35)   soul. It is an attribute of God. Our love.
CHILD: And did I love you?
FAUSTUS: Oh, my son.
CHILD: Tell me of love.
FAUSTUS: …no, can you doubt me?

(40) CHILD: I am unfitted to perceive duplicity
    [dishonesty]. I ask as for a gift.
FAUSTUS: Yes, I shall tell you of love.
CHILD: In this particular: the better to fit me to
    plead your case. It is the hour of audience.
(45) FAUSTUS: Yes.
CHILD: When the bell toll, and until the bell
    cease. And the gates have closed.
FAUSTUS: A man, a family begs to be
    reunited. In love…you wrote of it.

From David Mamet's FAUSTUS, © 2004

2. Based on the excerpt, where is this conversation most likely taking place?

The conversation is likely taking place

(1) in Faustus' home
(2) in the Child's yard
(3) before the gates of heaven
(4) in a dream
(5) in a church

3. Which of the following best describes what Faustus most wants?

Faustus wants

(1) to praise God
(2) his family to return to earth
(3) pity from the child
(4) the child to know him
(5) his son to return to him and his wife

4. Which of the following phrases best describes Faustus?

(1) daring and brave
(2) loving and pleading
(3) malicious and hurtful
(4) demanding and menacing
(5) weak and whining

Characters

Drama

① Learn the Skill

Characters are the fictional people who take part in a play. They are portrayed by actors. The action centers around the **protagonist**, or main character. Often, information about characters is revealed through their **dialogue**, or speeches, as well as through **stage directions** that describe actions and setting.

② Practice the Skill

By learning about characters, you will improve your study and test-taking skills, especially as they relate to the GED Language Arts/Reading Test. Read the excerpt and strategies below. Then answer the question that follows.

Ⓐ To understand Kate as a character, examine Kate's dialogue and the words she uses to describe herself. From this description, we learn that Kate is a young lawyer.

Ⓑ Think about reasons why Samantha might not believe Muffet. What does this tell you about Samantha's character?

Ⓒ Stage directions, which appear in parentheses in this book, give direction for the actors. They can also tell you more about a character's personality.

HOW ARE THE WOMEN'S PERSONALITIES DIFFERENT?

HOLLY: Katie. How long are you in town for?
KATE: I don't know. I'm here for a women-and-law conference.
Ⓐ Very grown-up, huh? I am now the young spokesperson at all the obligatory boring occasions.
(5) HOLLY: How's Robert?
SAMANTHA: Oh, he's fine. He was just cast in a TV pilot. He plays the male ingénue, and he's worried 'cause his hair-line is receding.
KATE: Holly, I forgot to tell you. Rita's coming down from
(10) Vermont. She told Samantha she had a six-year itch to see us all again.
SAMANTHA: Muffy wrote me and said that Rita was so fat at her wedding that she couldn't even walk down the aisle.
Ⓑ She had to be lowered to the altar by a crane. *(Pauses.)* I
(15) don't believe that.
Ⓒ MUFFET *(enters and joins the conversation immediately)*: Rita was a rotunda. It was pathetic when the orchestra played…*(Begins to sing "More.")* She must sit in bed and eat bonbons all day.

From Wendy Wasserstein's UNCOMMON WOMEN AND OTHERS, ©1978

✔ TEST-TAKING TIPS

To learn about one character, look for clues in the dialogue from other characters. Think about the information given about Rita.

1. Which phrase best describes Muffet?

    (1) a powerful business woman
    (2) a woman who gossips
    (3) an easygoing friend
    (4) a woman complimentary toward everyone
    (5) a rigid woman who follows orders

UNIT 4

③ Apply the Skill

Directions: Choose the <u>one best answer</u> to each question.

<u>Questions 2 through 4</u> refer to the following excerpt.

IS LIZA A WORLDLY WOMAN?

LIZA: How much?

TAXIMAN (*indicating the taximeter*): Can't you read? A shilling.

LIZA: A shilling for two minutes!!

(5)　TAXIMAN: Two minutes or ten: it's all the same.

LIZA: Well, I don't call it right.

TAXIMAN: Ever been in a taxi before?

LIZA (*with dignity*): Hundreds and thousands of

(10)　　times, young man.

TAXIMAN (*laughing at her*): Good for you, Judy. Keep the shilling, darling, with best love from all at home. Good luck! (*He drives off*).

(15)　LIZA (*humiliated*): Impidence!

(*She picks up the basket and trudges up the alley with it to her lodging: a small room with very old wall paper hanging loose in the damp places. A broken pane in the*

(20)　*window is mended with paper. A portrait of a popular actor and a fashion plate of ladies' dresses, all wildly beyond poor Eliza's means, both torn from newspapers, are pinned up on the wall. A birdcage*

(25)　*hangs in the window; but its tenant died long ago: it remains as a memorial only. These are the only visible luxuries: the rest is the irreducible minimum of poverty's needs: a wretched bed heaped with all*

(30)　*sorts of coverings that have any warmth in them, a draped packing case with a basin and jug on it and a little looking glass over it, a chair and table, the refuse of some suburban kitchen, and an American alarum*

(35)　*clock on the shelf above the unused fireplace: the whole lighted with a gas lamp with a penny in the slot meter. Rent: four shillings a week.*)

From George Bernard Shaw's PYGMALION, © 1913

2. Based on the excerpt, why is Liza most likely concerned about the cost of the taxi (line 1)?

Liza asks about the cost of the taxi ride because she

(1) wants to continue talking to the taximan
(2) is double-checking the taximeter
(3) cannot believe the cost of such a short ride
(4) cannot read the taximeter
(5) thinks the fare should be more expensive

3. Which of the following best describes Liza?

(1) fashionable
(2) impoverished
(3) sentimental
(4) meek
(5) jovial

4. Why is the direction line "Rent: four shillings a week" (lines 37–38) important in understanding Liza's overall character?

The line is important because it shows that

(1) she is capable of living well
(2) money is irrelevant to Liza's lifestyle
(3) Liza is striving for something more
(4) Liza has to carefully account for every cent she spends
(5) her apartment is reasonably priced compared to how much money she makes

Motivation

Drama

1 Learn the Skill

A character's **motivation** is the reason why he or she behaves in particular ways. Motivation can reveal a character's inner beliefs or convictions. Motivations can be explained by the character's words as well as his or her actions.

2 Practice the Skill

By analyzing a character's motivation, you will improve your study and test-taking skills, especially as they relate to the GED Language Arts/Reading Test. Read the excerpt and strategies below. Then answer the question that follows.

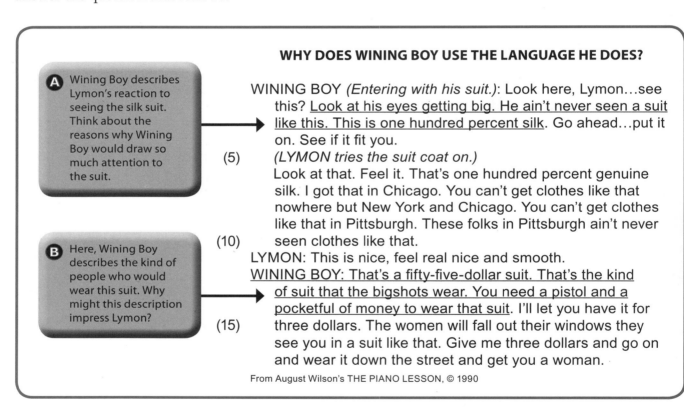

WHY DOES WINING BOY USE THE LANGUAGE HE DOES?

A Wining Boy describes Lymon's reaction to seeing the silk suit. Think about the reasons why Wining Boy would draw so much attention to the suit.

WINING BOY *(Entering with his suit.)*: Look here, Lymon…see this? Look at his eyes getting big. He ain't never seen a suit like this. This is one hundred percent silk. Go ahead…put it on. See if it fit you.
(5)
(LYMON tries the suit coat on.)
Look at that. Feel it. That's one hundred percent genuine silk. I got that in Chicago. You can't get clothes like that nowhere but New York and Chicago. You can't get clothes like that in Pittsburgh. These folks in Pittsburgh ain't never
(10) seen clothes like that.
LYMON: This is nice, feel real nice and smooth.
WINING BOY: That's a fifty-five-dollar suit. That's the kind of suit that the bigshots wear. You need a pistol and a pocketful of money to wear that suit. I'll let you have it for
(15) three dollars. The women will fall out their windows they see you in a suit like that. Give me three dollars and go on and wear it down the street and get you a woman.

B Here, Wining Boy describes the kind of people who would wear this suit. Why might this description impress Lymon?

From August Wilson's THE PIANO LESSON, © 1990

USING LOGIC

Examine Wining Boy's last section of dialogue. Determine if Wining Boy thinks Lymon would look good in the suit, or if he has another reason.

1. Which of the following best describes Wining Boy's true motivation for wanting to sell Lymon the suit?

He wants to sell Lymon the suit because

(1) it is one hundred percent genuine silk
(2) Lymon can't buy clothes like the suit in Pittsburgh
(3) he wants to make money
(4) he wants Lymon to get a woman
(5) he knows Lymon will think the suit is nice

③ Apply the Skill

Directions: Choose the one best answer to each question.

Questions 2 through 5 refer to the following excerpt.

WHAT IS MOTIVATING CYRANO?

LE BRET *(shrugging his shoulders)*: So be it! But tell me the real motive of your hatred for Silenus!

(5) CYRANO *(rising)*: That Silenus, so corpulent that he cannot reach below his belt, still believes himself dangerously attractive to the women; and rolls his great frogs' eyes at them, while he stammers through the play! And I have hated him since he
(10) allowed his glance one evening to fall upon her—Oh! I thought I saw a long slug crawling over a flower!

LE BRET *(dumbfounded)*: Eh? What? Can it be possible?

(15) CYRANO *(with a bitter laugh)*: That I should be in love? *(Changing his tone and speaking gravely.)* I am in love.

LE BRET: May I know? Have you never told me?

(20) CYRANO: Whom I love? Think of it. That nose, which is a quarter of an hour ahead of me everywhere I go, forbids me to dream of being loved even by the plainest, so whom do I love? A matter of course! I love—I
(25) couldn't help it!—the loveliest of all!

LE BRET: The loveliest?

CYRANO: Simply the loveliest in the world! The most brilliant, the most clever *(despondently)*, the fairest!

(30) LE BRET: Heavens, who is this woman?

CYRANO: A mortal danger without intending to be so, exquisite without dreaming of it, a snare of nature, a musk rose where love is held in ambush! Whoever knows her smile
(35) has known perfection. She is nothing if not graceful, her slightest gesture is wholly divine. And thou, O Venus, couldst never mount thy boat of shell, or thou, O Diana, stride through the mighty forests full of
(40) bloom, as she ascends her Sedan chair or glides along the Paris streets.

From Edmond Rostand's CYRANO DE BERGERAC, © 1931

2. What motivates Cyrano to change his tone when he tells Le Bret he is in love (line 17)?

Cyrano changes his tone because he

(1) thinks falling in love is a grave matter
(2) believes he will be in danger if he falls in love
(3) has low self-esteem regarding love
(4) loves a woman who deserves more than he thinks he has to offer
(5) is embarrassed to discuss his love with Le Bret

3. Why does Cyrano hate Silenus?

(1) Silenus is rude to Le Bret.
(2) Silenus is Cyrano's competition in the play.
(3) Silenus has looked at the woman Cyrano loves.
(4) Silenus is more attractive than Cyrano.
(5) Cyrano thinks Silenus lacks talent.

4. Which of the following is similar to the way in which Cyrano describes his love?

(1) An art critic describes a masterpiece.
(2) A teacher describes her poorest student.
(3) A writer describes his revisions.
(4) An architect describes a dilapidated building.
(5) A coffee lover describes weak coffee.

5. Later in the play, Cyrano helps another character, Christian, win the affection of the woman by writing love letters for him. Based on the information from the excerpt, which of the following is most likely his motivation for helping Christian?

(1) Cyrano actually does not like the woman.
(2) Cyrano feels that his nose makes him so ugly the woman could not possibly love him.
(3) Christian is Cyrano's brother.
(4) Le Bret has told Cyrano he must help Christian.
(5) Cyrano decides to become a priest.

Theme

Drama

① Learn the Skill

The **theme** is the central or overall idea of a dramatic work. A theme is different from the plot of the play. A play's theme is usually not directly stated, so the reader must interpret verbal and nonverbal cues presented in the play and then make inferences about the ideas the playwright is trying to express. Adding these ideas together can lead the reader to understand the theme of the play.

② Practice the Skill

By mastering how to identify the theme, you will improve your study and test-taking skills, especially as they relate to the GED Language Arts/Reading Test. Read the excerpt and strategies below. Then answer the question that follows.

A Meridian's first line indicates that he and Lorenzo have been discussing their friend Parnell. Examine the way Meridian describes Parnell.

B Lorenzo and Meridian have different ideas about how much to trust people. Think about this debate and how it relates to Meridian's earlier lines.

IS PARNELL CONSIDERED A FRIEND?

MERIDIAN: But I think that Parnell has proven to be a pretty
A good friend to all of us. He's the only white man in this town
who ever really stuck his neck out in order to do—to do
right. He's *fought* to bring about his trial—I can't tell you
(5) how hard he's fought. If it weren't for him, there'd be much
less hope.
B **LORENZO:** I guess I'm just not as nice as you are. I don't trust
as many people as you trust.
MERIDIAN: We can't afford to become too distrustful, Lorenzo.
(10) **LORENZO:** We can't afford to be too trusting, either. See, when
a white man's a *good* white man, he's good because he
wants *you* to be good. Well, sometimes I just might want to
be *bad*. I got as much right to be bad as anybody else.
MERIDIAN: No, you don't.
(15) **LORENZO:** Why not?
MERIDIAN: Because you know better.

From James Baldwin's BLUES FOR MISTER CHARLIE, © 1964

USING LOGIC

Determining the main idea of the play can help you discover the play's theme. In this scene, the main idea is that different people have different opinions about how much to trust.

1. Which of the following best describes the theme of this scene?

   (1) Parnell cannot be trusted.
   (2) Some people feel they cannot trust people of other backgrounds.
   (3) Lawyers cannot be trusted.
   (4) Trust should be given freely to everyone.
   (5) Some people are not to be trusted.

Directions: Choose the one best answer to each question.

Questions 2 through 4 refer to the following excerpt.

WHAT IS MR. FRANK'S MESSAGE TO ANNE?

MR. FRANK: There's something more. Go on. Look further.
(He goes over to the sink, pouring a glass of milk from a thermos bottle.)

(5) ANNE *(Pulling out a past-board bound book)*: A diary! *(She throws her arms around her father)* I've never had a diary. And I've always longed for one. *(She looks around the room)* Pencil, pencil, pencil, pencil.

(10) *(She starts down the stairs)* I'm going down to the office to get a pencil.

MR. FRANK: Anne! No! *(He goes after her, catching her by the arm and pulling her back.)*

(15) ANNE *(Startled)*: But there's no one in the building now.

MR. FRANK: It doesn't matter. I don't want you ever to go beyond that door.

ANNE *(Sobered)*: Never…? Not even at

(20) nighttime, when everyone is gone? Or on Sundays? Can't I go down to listen to the radio?

MR FRANK: Never. I am sorry, Anneke. It isn't safe. No, you must never go beyond that

(25) door. *(For the first time ANNE realizes what "going into hiding" means.)*

ANNE: I see.

MR. FRANK: It'll be hard, I know. But always remember this, Anneke. There are no

(30) walls, there are no bolts, no locks that anyone can put on your mind. Miep will bring us books. We will read history, poetry, mythology. *(He gives her the glass of milk)* Here's your milk. *(With his*

(35) *arm about her, they go over to the couch, sitting down side by side)* As a matter of fact, between us, Anne, being here has certain advantages for you. For instance, you remember the battle you had with your

(40) mother the other day on the subject of overshoes? You said you'd rather die than wear overshoes? But in the end you had to wear them? Well now, you see, for as long as we are here you will never have to wear

(45) overshoes! Isn't that good? And the coat that you inherited from Margot, you won't have to wear that any more. And the piano! You won't have to practice on the piano. I tell you, this is going to be a fine life

(50) for you!

From Frances Goodrich and Albert Hackett's THE DIARY OF ANNE FRANK, © 1956

2. What is the most likely reason that Mr. Frank will not allow Anne to go to the office to get a pencil for her diary (lines 12–14)?

   (1) Mr. Frank does not want Anne to go to the office by herself.
   (2) Mr. Frank wants to finish his conversation with Anne before she gets a pencil.
   (3) Mr. Frank has a pencil for Anne already.
   (4) Mr. Frank does not appreciate Anne's eagerness to write in her diary.
   (5) Mr. Frank knows it is too dangerous for Anne to leave the apartment.

3. Which of the following best describes the theme of this excerpt?

   (1) Even in difficult times, small joys can be found.
   (2) Stories are the key to happiness.
   (3) Gifts from the heart are the most important kind.
   (4) A person cannot fear what he or she cannot see.
   (5) Knowledge will overcome everything.

4. To what can the gift of Anne's diary be compared?

   (1) a cup of soup given to a sick friend
   (2) a DVD given to a movie enthusiast
   (3) an easel given to an established artist
   (4) a new guitar given to a poor musician
   (5) a cookbook given to a chef

UNIT 4

Tone

Drama

① Learn the Skill

Playwrights use details to set the **tone**, or attitude, of a play. Tone can be displayed through the use of sarcasm, anger, fear, humor, or a combination of these elements. Tone is often described in emotional words, such as "The character's tone is very sad." As you read a play, examine the feelings that are evoked from the character's actions and dialogue as well as the plot.

② Practice the Skill

By analyzing the tone of a play, you will improve your study and test-taking skills, especially as they relate to the GED Language Arts/Reading Test. Read the excerpt and strategies below. Then answer the question that follows.

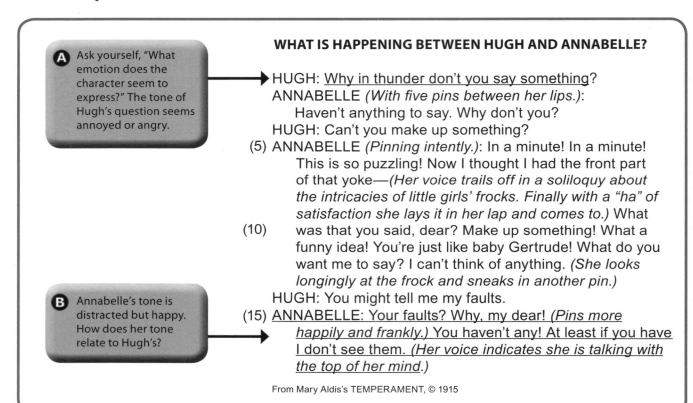

A Ask yourself, "What emotion does the character seem to express?" The tone of Hugh's question seems annoyed or angry.

B Annabelle's tone is distracted but happy. How does her tone relate to Hugh's?

WHAT IS HAPPENING BETWEEN HUGH AND ANNABELLE?

HUGH: <u>Why in thunder don't you say something</u>?
ANNABELLE *(With five pins between her lips.)*:
    Haven't anything to say. Why don't you?
HUGH: Can't you make up something?
(5) ANNABELLE *(Pinning intently.)*: In a minute! In a minute!
    This is so puzzling! Now I thought I had the front part
    of that yoke—*(Her voice trails off in a soliloquy about
    the intricacies of little girls' frocks. Finally with a "ha" of
    satisfaction she lays it in her lap and comes to.)* What
(10)   was that you said, dear? Make up something! What a
    funny idea! You're just like baby Gertrude! What do you
    want me to say? I can't think of anything. *(She looks
    longingly at the frock and sneaks in another pin.)*
HUGH: You might tell me my faults.
(15) <u>ANNABELLE: Your faults? Why, my dear!</u> *(Pins more
    happily and frankly.)* <u>You haven't any! At least if you have
    I don't see them.</u> *(Her voice indicates she is talking with
    the top of her mind.)*

From Mary Aldis's TEMPERAMENT, © 1915

✔ **TEST-TAKING TIPS**

Watch for italicized stage direction. These notes often give the reader clues for interpreting a character's feelings and tone.

1. What best describes Hugh's tone?

    (1) emotionless
    (2) sad
    (3) aggravated
    (4) elated
    (5) threatened

Directions: Choose the <u>one best answer</u> to each question.

<u>Questions 2 through 4</u> refer to the following excerpt.

IS JACK PLEASED WITH ALGERNON?

ALGERNON: What a fearful liar you are, Jack. I have not been called back to town at all.

JACK: Yes, you have.

ALGERNON: I haven't heard any one
(5)   call me.

JACK: Your duty as a gentleman calls you back.

ALGERNON: My duty as a gentleman has never interfered with my pleasures in the
(10)   smallest degree.

JACK: I can quite understand that.

ALGERNON: Well, Cecily is a darling.

JACK: You are not to talk of Miss Cardew like that. I don't like it.

(15) ALGERNON: Well, I don't like your clothes. You look perfectly ridiculous in them. Why on earth don't you go up and change? It is perfectly childish to be in deep mourning for a man who is actually staying for a
(20)   whole week with you in your house as a guest. I call it grotesque.

JACK: You are certainly not staying with me for a whole week as a guest or anything else. You have got to leave…by the four-
(25)   five train.

ALGERNON: I certainly won't leave you so long as you are in mourning. It would be most unfriendly. If I were in mourning you would stay with me, I suppose. I should
(30)   think it very unkind if you didn't.

JACK: Well, will you go if I change my clothes?

ALGERNON: Yes, If you are not too long. I never saw anybody take so long to dress, and with such little result.

(35) JACK: Well, at any rate, that is better than being always over-dressed as you are.

ALGERNON: If I am occasionally a little over-dressed, I make up for it by being always immensely over-educated.

(40) JACK: Your vanity is ridiculous, your conduct an outrage, and your presence in my garden utterly absurd. However, you have got to catch the four-five, and I hope you will have a pleasant journey back to town.

From Oscar Wilde's THE IMPORTANCE OF BEING EARNEST, © 1899

2. What do Jack's words indicate?

Jack is a

(1) patient man
(2) man with a good sense of humor
(3) protective man
(4) gracious host
(5) bitter man

3. What is Algernon's tone?

(1) happy
(2) sarcastic
(3) angry
(4) conceited
(5) modest

4. How might the feeling of the excerpt be described?

The feeling of the excerpt is

(1) friendly
(2) angry
(3) sad
(4) loving
(5) mournful

Mood

Drama

① Learn the Skill

A play's **mood** is related to the tone. The mood of a play is its emotional atmosphere. Mood can be determined by descriptive words in a character's dialogue or in stage direction, which can help illustrate feelings.

② Practice the Skill

By learning how to determine a play's mood, you will improve your study and test-taking skills, especially as they relate to the GED Language Arts/Reading Test. Read the excerpt and strategies below. Then answer the question that follows.

WHAT ROLE DO THE CITIZENS PLAY?

A The tone of the citizens helps to set the mood of the scene.

B Both Capulet and Montague are angry as they call for their swords. Think about how the characters' words and actions might affect the mood of the play.

A <u>CITIZENS OF THE WATCH: Clubs, bills [broad-tipped spears] and partisans! Strike! Beat them down! Down with the Capulets. Down with the Montagues.</u>
(Enter old CAPULET *in his gown, and his* WIFE)
(5) CAPULET: What noise is this? Give me my long sword, ho!
CAPULET'S WIFE: A crutch, a crutch—why call for
    a sword?
B *(Enter old* MONTAGUE *(with his sword drawn)*, *and his* WIFE)
(10) CAPULET: My sword, I say. Old Montague is come,
    And flourishes his blade in spite [defiance] of me.
MONTAGUE: Thou villain Capulet! *(His* WIFE *holds him back)* Hold me not, let me go.
MONTAGUE'S WIFE: Thou shalt not stir one foot to seek
(15)   a foe.

From William Shakespeare's ROMEO AND JULIET

💡 USING LOGIC

Often the mood of a scene can provide clues for a reader about upcoming events. Based on the mood of this excerpt, you can guess that the rest of the play will involve violence between the Montagues and Capulets.

1. What is the mood between Capulet and Montague?

   (1) rage
   (2) serenity
   (3) indifference
   (4) mild tension
   (5) kinship

UNIT 4

Directions: Choose the <u>one best answer</u> to each question.

<u>Questions 2 through 4</u> refer to the following excerpt.

WHAT DOES THE DIALOGUE BETWEEN BRICK AND MARGARET SUGGEST?

BRICK: I've dropped my crutch.
 (He has stopped rubbing his hair dry but sill stands hanging onto the towel rack in a white towel-cloth robe.)
(5) MARGARET: Lean on me.
BRICK: No, just give me my crutch.
MARGARET: Lean on my shoulder.
BRICK: *I don't want to lean on your shoulder, I want my crutch!*
(10) *(This is spoken like sudden lightning.)*
 Are you going to give me my crutch or do I have to get down on my knees on the floor and—
MARGARET: *Here, here, take it, take it!*
(15) *(She has thrust the crutch at him.)*
BRICK (hobbling out): Thanks…
MARGARET: We musn't scream at each other, the walls in this house have ears…
 —but that's the first time I've heard you
(20) raise your voice in a long time, Brick. A crack in the wall?—Of composure?—I think that's a good sign…
 A sign of nerves in a player on the defensive!
(25) *(Brick turns and smiles at her coolly over his fresh drink.)*
BRICK: It just hasn't happened yet, Maggie.
MARGARET: What?
BRICK: The click I get in my head when
(30) I've had enough of this stuff to make me peaceful…
 Will you do me a favor?
MARGARET: Maybe I will. What favor?
BRICK: Just, just keep your voice down!
(35) MARGARET: *(in a hoarse whisper)*: I'll do that favor, I'll speak in a whisper, if not shut up completely, if you will do me a favor and make that drink your last one till after the party.

(40) BRICK: What party?
MARGARET: Big Daddy's birthday party.
BRICK: Is this Big Daddy's birthday?
MARGARET: You know this is Big Daddy's birthday!
(45) BRICK: No, I don't, I forgot it.
MARGARET: Well, I remembered if for you…
 (They are both speaking as breathlessly as a pair of kids after a fight, drawing deep exhausted breaths and looking at
(50) *each other with faraway eyes, shaking and panting together as if they had broken apart from a violent struggle.)*

From Tennessee Williams' CAT ON A HOT TIN ROOF, © 1955

2. Which of the following best describes the mood of the excerpt?

 (1) sincere
 (2) loving
 (3) hostile
 (4) regretful
 (5) jovial

3. Based on the stage directions, which of the following best describes Brick's character?

 Brick is

 (1) warm
 (2) ambivalent
 (3) meek
 (4) bad-tempered
 (5) sullen

4. Why does Margaret think it is a good sign that Brick has raised his voice (lines 20–22)?

 Margaret thinks it is good that Brick has raised his voice because he is

 (1) showing emotion
 (2) demonstrating authority
 (3) becoming more human
 (4) gaining his strength
 (5) overcoming shyness

UNIT 4

Unit 4 Review

The Unit Review is structured to resemble the GED Language Arts/Reading Test. Be sure to read each question and all possible answers carefully before answering. To record your answers, fill in the numbered circle that corresponds to the answer you select for each question. Make no stray or unnecessary marks. If you change an answer, erase your first mark completely. Mark only one answer space for each question; multiple answers will be scored as incorrect.

Sample Question
Which of the following words best describes Oscar?

(1) slovenly
(2) angry
(3) happy
(4) steady
(5) silly

① ● ③ ④ ⑤

Questions 1 through 6 refer to the following excerpt.

HOW ARE THE CHARACTERS IN THIS SCENE DIFFERENT?

OSCAR: Deal the cards!
MURRAY: What did you do that for?
OSCAR: Just deal the cards. You want to play poker, deal the cards. You want
(5)   to eat, go to Schrafft's. *(To VINNIE.)* Keep your sandwich and your pickles to yourself. I'm losing ninety-two dollars and everybody's getting fat! *(He screams.)*
Felix!
(10) *(FELIX appears in the kitchen doorway.)*
FELIX: What?
OSCAR: Close the kitchen and sit down. It's a quarter to twelve. I still got an hour and a half to win this month's alimony.
(15) ROY *(sniffs)*: What is that smell? Disinfectant! *(He smells the cards.)* It's the cards. He washed the cards! *(He throws down the cards, takes his jacket from the chair, and moves past the table*
(20) *to put his money into the kitty box.)*
FELIX *(comes to the table with OSCAR'S drink, which he puts down; then he sits in his own seat)*: Okay. What's the bet?
OSCAR *(hurrying to his seat)*: I can't believe
(25)   it. We're gonna play cards again. *(He sits.)* It's up to Roy. Roy, baby, what are you gonna do?
ROY: I'm gonna get in a cab and go to Central Park. If I don't get some fresh air,
(30)   you got yourself a dead accountant. *(He moves toward the door.)*

OSCAR *(follows him)*: What do you mean? It's not even twelve o'clock.
ROY *(turns back to OSCAR)*: Look, I've been
(35)   sitting here breathing Lysol and ammonia for four hours! Nature didn't intend for poker to be played like that. *(He crosses to the door.)* If you wanna have a game next week *(He points to FELIX.)* either
(40)   Louis Pasteur cleans up after we've gone, or we play in the Hotel Dixie! Good night!
(He goes and slams the door. There is a moment's silence. OSCAR goes back to
(45) *the table and sits.)*
OSCAR: We got just enough for handball!
FELIX: Gee, I'm sorry. Is it my fault?
VINNIE: No, I guess no one feels like playing much lately.
(50) MURRAY: Yeah. I don't know what it is, but something's happening to the old gang. *(He goes to a side chair, sits and puts on his shoes.)*
OSCAR: Don't you know what's happening
(55)   to the old gang? It's breaking up. Everyone's getting divorced. I swear, we used to have better games when we couldn't get out at night.

From Neil Simon's THE ODD COUPLE, © 1965

1. What is Oscar's mood in the excerpt?

   (1) anxious
   (2) irritated
   (3) excited
   (4) sad
   (5) complex

   ① ② ③ ④ ⑤

2. What is the overall theme of this excerpt?

   (1) Old friendships are better than new ones.
   (2) Playing poker with the guys is more fun than going on a date.
   (3) As people change, sometimes so do rituals and friendships.
   (4) Neatness should take precedence over a game of cards.
   (5) Friends may get angry at one another, but in the end, they will always be around.

   ① ② ③ ④ ⑤

3. If Felix were to go on a date, which of the following activities would he most likely choose to do?

   He would choose to go to a

   (1) loud, action-filled movie
   (2) dusty baseball game
   (3) notoriously messy friend's house to socialize with other people
   (4) very clean restaurant with excellent reviews
   (5) park to walk while holding hands

   ① ② ③ ④ ⑤

4. Why did Roy leave the poker game?

   (1) The place is too clean, and he cannot breathe due to the smell of disinfectant.
   (2) He is losing all of his money and wants to take a walk instead.
   (3) He is angry at Oscar for wanting to continue the card game while Felix is in the kitchen.
   (4) The other men are making fun of him for being tired so early.
   (5) He would rather go to Central Park than play poker.

   ① ② ③ ④ ⑤

5. Which of the following best describes Felix?

   Felix is

   (1) messy
   (2) delighted
   (3) sincere
   (4) disgusted
   (5) quiet

   ① ② ③ ④ ⑤

6. Which of the following most likely happens immediately after this excerpt?

   (1) The four men play poker as though nothing has happened.
   (2) Oscar gets up and cleans around Roy's seat.
   (3) Oscar and Felix have an argument about Oscar's messy ways.
   (4) The four men clean up the poker table.
   (5) Vinnie and Murray leave.

   ① ② ③ ④ ⑤

Questions 7 through 14 refer to the following excerpt.

WHAT IS IMPORTANT TO THIS FAMILY?

SHPRINTZE: Mama, where should we put these?

GOLDE: Put them on my head! By the stove, foolish girl. Where is Chava?

(5) HODEL: She's in the barn, milking.

BIELKE: When will Papa be home?

GOLDE: It's almost Sabbath and he worries a lot when he'll be home! All day long riding on top of his wagon like a prince.

(10) TZEITEL: Mama, you know that Papa works hard.

GOLDE: His horse works harder! And you don't have to defend your papa to me. I know him a little longer than you. He

(15) could drive a person crazy. *(Under her breath.)* He should only live and be well. *(Out loud.)* Shprintze, bring me some more potatoes.

(CHAVA enters carrying a basket, with a

(20) *book under her apron.)* Chava, did you finish milking?

CHAVA: Yes, Mama. *(She drops the book.)*

GOLDE: You were reading again? Why does a girl have to read? Will it get her a better

(25) husband? Here. *(Hands CHAVA the book.)*

(CHAVA exits into the house. SHPRINTZE enters with a basket of potatoes.)

(30) SHPRINTZE: Mama, Yente's coming. She's down the road.

HODEL: Maybe she's finally found a good match for you, Tzeitzel.

GOLDE: From your mouth to God's ears.

(35) TZEITEL: Why does she have to come now? It's almost Sabbath.

GOLDE: Go finish in the barn. I want to talk to Yente alone.

SHPRINTZE: Mama, can I go out and play?

(40) GOLDE: You have feet? Go.

BIELKE: Can I go too?

GOLDE: Go too.

(SHPRINTZE and BIELKE exit.)

TZEITEL: But Mama, the men she finds. The

(45) last one was so old and he was bald. He had no hair.

GOLDE: A poor girl without a dowry can't be so particular. You want hair, marry a monkey.

(50) TZEITEL: After all, Mama, I'm not yet twenty years old, and—

GOLDE: Shah! *(Spits between her fingers.)* Do you have to boast about your age? Do you want to tempt the Evil Eye?

(55) Inside.

(TZEITEL leaves the kitchen as YENTE enters from outside.)

YENTE: Golde darling, I had to see you because I have such news for you. And

(60) not just every-day-in-the-week news— once-in-a-lifetime news. And where are your daughters? Outside, no? Good. Such diamonds, such jewels. You'll see, Golde, I'll find everyone of them a

(65) husband. But you shouldn't be so picky. Even the worst husband, God forbid, is better than no husband, God forbid. And who should know better than me? Ever since my husband died I've been a poor

(70) widow, alone, nobody to talk to, nothing to say to anyone. It's no life. All I do at night is think of him, and even thinking of him gives me no pleasure, because you know as well as I, he was not much of a

(75) person. Never made a living, everything he touched turned to mud, but better than nothing.

From Joseph Stein's FIDDLER ON THE ROOF, © 1964

7. Which of the following best describes what Golde most wants?

Golde wants

(1) her husband to return home from work
(2) her daughter Chava to stop reading so much
(3) her children to work more and play less
(4) her daughters to marry
(5) to have a quiet conversation with Yente

①②③④⑤

8. Based on Golde's response to Shprintze's question in lines 1 through 4, how might you describe Golde?

Golde is

(1) feisty
(2) quiet
(3) sarcastic
(4) a jokester
(5) thoughtless

①②③④⑤

9. Which of the following best describes Yente's feelings about her news?

(1) nervous
(2) mournful
(3) excited
(4) annoyed
(5) triumphant

①②③④⑤

10. What might be Golde's motivation for spitting between her fingers (line 52)?

Golde spits between her fingers as a

(1) punishment toward Tzeitel
(2) cursing gesture
(3) gesture of fun loving
(4) superstitious gesture
(5) way to indicate that she wants to be left alone

①②③④⑤

11. Which phrase best describes Yente?

(1) a solemn widow
(2) an active busy-body
(3) an irritated neighbor
(4) a fretful worrier
(5) a woman with a large ego

①②③④⑤

12. Based on the excerpt, which of the following jobs might Chava want to pursue?

(1) farmer
(2) matchmaker
(3) doctor
(4) seamstress
(5) librarian

①②③④⑤

13. What might be Golde's biggest complaint about Chava?

Golde might complain that Chava

(1) is not sufficiently interested in finding a good husband
(2) should not read while milking the cows
(3) is too clumsy
(4) does not do enough work around the house
(5) takes too long to finish her chores

①②③④⑤

14. How does Tzeitel feel about Yente's arrival?

(1) She is happy to welcome Yente.
(2) She worries that Yente has not found her a suitable husband.
(3) She is afraid that Yente might have found another bald man for her to marry.
(4) She is irritated because she does not want to marry yet.
(5) She worries that Golde will be disappointed with Yente's news.

①②③④⑤

Answer Key

UNIT 1 NON-FICTION

LESSON 1, pp. 2–3
1. Analysis: (5), The phrase "finds that its teachers are in fact more effective than those with traditional training" supports the idea that Teach for America teachers are valuable.
2. Comprehension: (5), The subject line of the memorandum and the second paragraph tell us that the human resources director wants to clarify dress code for the upcoming summer season.
3. Application: (3), Based on the list of bulleted items, an office manager could ask employees not to wear shirts with offensive slogans.

LESSON 2, pp. 4–5
1. Analysis: (4), The question asks you to use the summary to evaluate Bruce Wayne as a young adult. Answer 4 best summarizes how Wayne feels about formal education.
2. Analysis: (5), In lines 3 through 5, the speaker says he has been "granted the role of defending freedom in its hour of maximum danger."
3. Comprehension: (1), The speaker is asking his listeners to think about what they can do to help their country. Answer 1 best summarizes this statement.
4. Comprehension: (4), In lines 4 through 6, the speaker states that the "political thing to do…is to either ignore them or deny them."
5. Synthesis: (3), The speaker concludes his speech by saying that he believes "that the people have got to have confidence in the…men who run for office." Answer 3 best summarizes this statement.

LESSON 3, pp. 6–7
1. Comprehension: (5), The passage states that the Mazda 6 matches up with "rivals in the mid-size segment."
2. Analysis: (2), Eric Jackson would be best placed in the category of option 2 because his salary falls within the approved salary range.
3. Comprehension: (4), The letter states that a condition such as a down payment may lower the required monthly payments.

LESSON 4, pp. 8–9
1. Analysis: (3), The speaker says that his work week begins on Thursday, and that on Thursdays, he patrols the roads and walks the trails.

2. Comprehension: (2), The author explains in paragraph 3 that he began to teach poetry as a way to get the attention of a new fourth grade class in April. The passage states that the teacher was working in a segregated school in Boston that was crowded and poor, which indicates that it was not a suburban school. And while the teacher was fired in the spring, it was for teaching poems that were not approved. "Teaching poetry" alone was not enough of a reason to fire the teacher.
3. Analysis: (1), In paragraph 4, the author explains that the poem he read to his students was not on the list of approved "fourth grade poems."
4. Synthesis: (2), The author means that the results of the first tests gave him an idea about how the constant change of teachers affected the students. In lines 15 through 17, the author gives details showing how poorly the students were doing.
5. Analysis: (3), Because the author is a teacher, it is logical to assume that he most likely went on to teach at a different school.

LESSON 5, pp. 10–11
1. Comprehension: (4), The first paragraph explains that global warming has many effects, such as hunger, thirst, floods, and disease. The author lists all of the effects before the cause.
2. Comprehension: (2), The first line of the article explains that scientists who conducted the study found that high-fructose corn syrup was a potential cause of weight gain.
3. Analysis: (4), The third paragraph explains how the process in which sugars are turned into fat increased significantly in those people who drank fructose drinks.
4. Analysis: (1), Lines 28 and 29 state that dieters should not eliminate fruit because it contains many beneficial nutrients.

LESSON 6, pp. 12–13
1. Synthesis: (1), The author states that "at first there is no discrimination in the eye," meaning that nothing stands out or calls attention to itself. Then he says that smaller things caught his attention.
2. Analysis: (2), The old policy allowed people to enter the building using different types of photo identification and allowed them to phone a supervisor if they forgot their badge. The new policy requires that people show a company badge to enter the business.
3. Application: (5), A child care facility is most likely to be interested in controlling the access of people entering a building, since its managers would be particularly interested in the safety of the children there.

LESSON 7, pp. 14–15
1. Analysis: (3), Answer 3 is the only option that gives insight into the author's beliefs about the subject. The other options are phrases that describe what happens in the movie.

UNIT 1 (continued)

2. Analysis: (2), This passage most clearly demonstrates the kinds of eating habits that are associated with country living. In the first paragraph, the author explains that the rural area that was studied had more convenience stores than grocery stores or supermarkets, and that those typically do not stock the healthy food found in grocery stores or supermarkets.

3. Analysis: (1), The author uses many facts and statistics throughout the excerpt, such as the percentage of convenience stores in Orangeburg County, and the percentage of stores in that county that carry fruits and vegetables.

4. Synthesis: (4), The author uses the phrase "food desert" to make a comparison. She says that, in the way that a desert has limits on the amount of water and resources it provides, a "food desert" has limits on the amount of healthy foods that are readily available to buy in that area.

LESSON 8, pp. 16–17

1. Analysis: (4), The author states that, "While Dudley has everything, including a spare bedroom for his toys, Harry is forced to live in a tiny space under the stairs" (lines 4–6). This line implies that Harry's Aunt Petunia and Uncle Vernon do not treat their nephew the same way they treat their son. In fact, they give him very little love and support as he is forced to live under the stairs while his cousin has an entire extra bedroom just for his toys.

2. Analysis: (2), Lines 11 and 12 refer to a "colorized version of *The Maltese Falcon*." Given that the author is writing about people who watch too much television, it can be implied based on these facts that *The Maltese Falcon* is a black-and-white movie.

3. Comprehension: (1), Answer 1 is the only option which is fully expressed in the excerpt.

4. Synthesis: (1), The author discusses how people used to be "fond of the outdoors" but now are content to stay inside.

LESSON 9, pp. 18–19

1. Comprehension: (5), The excerpt explains that gas is cheaper in Venezuela than it is in the United States. It also explains that in "most other industrialized nations," gas is more expensive than it is in the United States. So gas in the United States is more expensive than in some areas, but less expensive than in others.

2. Synthesis: (2), In lines 18 and 19, the author clearly states that sometimes separate is better. In the excerpt, she explains her belief that girls who are in a separate education system are more likely to do well on standardized tests and perform better in math and science. Answer 2 most accurately restates the author's words in the excerpt.

3. Analysis: (4), Line 29 says "The evidence, though scant, is promising." The rest of the paragraph goes on to say that the evidence includes higher test scores and better performance from the girls in the all-girls' classes.

4. Analysis: (1), Answer 1 is the only option that provides support for a conclusion.

LESSON 10, pp. 20–21

1. Analysis: (4), The author says that there is a clear need to look into a mining disaster. Later, the author implies that the mine operators could have prevented the disaster, but that they "concealed danger warnings and…chiseled underground pillar supports to the point of breaking." These statements show that the author believes people need to be aware of and try to change the way mine operators work.

2. Synthesis: (3), The excerpt's initial focus is on the National Park Service Centennial Initiative and the money that it would cost to enact it. At the end of the excerpt, the author encourages the legislature to provide the money for this initiative. Answer 3 best states the author's beliefs.

3. Synthesis: (2), Answer 2 best conveys the sense of urgency for immediate, positive action that the author expresses in the excerpt.

4. Synthesis: (1), In lines 11 and 12, the author states "the parks need all the help they can get." Throughout the excerpt, the author discusses ways in which the federal government could help the parks. Answer 1 best restates the author's point of view.

LESSON 11, pp. 22–23

1. Comprehension: (2), The author is emphasizing that her party is "the instrument of the people" and that people have turned to her party in times of need. She's encouraging people to do so again.

2. Analysis: (2), The author gives many facts and details about the financial state and the impact of taxes on the country. He delivers these details in a very straightforward, calm manner.

3. Analysis: (4), The first paragraph explains how the national budget is facing difficulties and gives specific examples about those problems. The author is not asking people for money, and his uncomfortable feeling concerns the good luck, or prosperity, the country is facing. He never mentions that people should begin to save money.

4. Analysis: (3), Answer 3 is the only option that advises readers to take action (to re-examine and determine if they are acting in a manner in which the Founders encouraged).

5. Synthesis: (1), The author uses straightforward, factual wording, so he is not writing in an ambiguous manner. While this excerpt does not advocate fighting of any kind, it does encourage action and change, so it is not peaceful. The author very clearly supports the people and ideals of his country, so the excerpt is not unpatriotic. Finally, the author does not provide insights from other points of view, so the excerpt is not balanced. The author does provide much information, so answer 1 is the best choice.

LESSON 12, pp. 24–25

1. Comprehension: (3), Lines 10 and 12 state that "[pit bulls] bite, hold, shake, and tear." Answer 3 is the only option that accurately rephrases the text into a generalization.

2. Comprehension: (1), The second paragraph indicates that the company has operated for 25 years.

3. Synthesis: (2), The first paragraph of the pamphlet sets out the company's attitude, which is that trees should be maintained in order to provide shade and comfort.

UNIT 1 (continued)

4. Application: (3), Removing limbs prevents future damage, just as a flu vaccination prevents future illness.

UNIT 1 REVIEW, pp. 26–29

1. Synthesis: (3), The excerpt mentions things that both Congress and state governments can do to improve the way the juvenile justice system deals with young offenders.

2. Analysis: (2), Lines 5 through 10 state that young offenders who are kept with adult offenders are "exposed to social pressures and develop personal contacts" and are more likely to become career criminals.

3. Analysis: (2), In lines 33 through 35, the author states a belief that too many children are being held for truancy. The author goes on to outline reasons why the detention of truancy offenders in juvenile centers is bad.

4. Comprehension: (1), Paragraph 3 outlines ways in which states could qualify for federal funding by certifying that young offenders are not being jailed as adults, except in cases of heinous crimes.

5. Synthesis: (4), Paragraph 6 states that "another cause for concern is the significant racial and ethnic disparities." Answer 4 is the only option that addresses racial inequality.

6. Comprehension: (3), The author states "I am writing to introduce myself to you and your associates" in line 1.

7. Synthesis: (4), The use of the phrase "preferred guests" indicates that the recipient is a special client of the hotel.

8. Analysis: (2), The letter is addressed to "Mr. Frank Thomas, CEO" of "Thomas Building Supplies."

9. Analysis: (5), The previous sentence refers to an event that Mr. Thomas's company is organizing in September and hints at other possible events in the future. The author wants to make sure that Mr. Thomas knows he can rely on her for assistance with those events.

10. Application: (3), The tone of the letter is professional and courteous, indicating that the author cares about her job and helping other people in ways related to that job.

UNIT 2 FICTION

LESSON 1, pp. 32–33

1. Analysis: (3), Lines 4 through 7 explain that nothing about the man's narrative changes. From this context, you can assume that the tone stays the same.

2. Application: (3), If you did not already know that *deserted* means "empty," you could guess its meaning from context clues. The narrator says "I remained alone in the bare carriage" (lines 13–14), so no other answer option fits.

3. Comprehension: (4), From the information that precedes the narrator "handing a shilling to a weary looking man," you can guess from context clues that the narrator is going through the gate to the bazaar. Based on this information, you can assume that a shilling is the price of entry to the bazaar.

4. Analysis: (1), The excerpt tells us that a town (hamlet) called Barry's Ford began where a river was "fordable" and that there is now a bridge there. From this information, you can assume that a *ford* is a "place to cross a river."

LESSON 2, pp. 34–35

1. Comprehension: (2), In lines 5 through 7, the narrator explains the strange feeling she gets from the house. She tells John about the feeling, but he believes she is simply cold.

2. Comprehension: (3), The beginning of the excerpt tells us that the plane has encountered heavy weather.

3. Analysis: (3), The narrator describes the dramatic way the plane is being tossed about in the heavy weather. The neighbor goes on to tell Francis about his life-long dream of owning a farm. You can assume he is afraid of the possibility that the plane might crash because of the bad weather.

4. Analysis: (5), Based on the context, you can assume that the term "painkiller" refers to the drink in the flask that is mentioned in lines 10 and 11.

5. Analysis: (4), Lines 23 through 25 explain that the landing "shook [the passengers] so violently" that an old man was hurt in the process.

LESSON 3, pp. 36–37

1. Comprehension: (5), Lines 9 through 11 explain that Susan tells jokes and riddles to get attention, while Emily is quiet and does not draw attention to herself.

2. Comprehension: (3), The excerpt explains that the couple do not enjoy the same kinds of music, so answer 1 is incorrect. The narrator does like bluegrass music, while Gloria does not, so answer 2 is incorrect. Gloria says she could see the narrator might like bebop music, in contrast to bluegrass, so answer 4 is incorrect. The husband is the only one who likes country music, so answer 5 is incorrect.

3. Analysis: (1), In lines 7 and 8, Gloria explains that hillbilly music and the New York Stock Exchange change quickly in a negative way: "If you see a sharp rise in it, you better watch out."

4. Analysis: (2), Earlier in the excerpt, the narrator says that his "perceptions were shaped in South Carolina." The author is showing the difference between Gloria's upbringing in the North and his own childhood in the South.

5. Application: (4), You can assume from the author's description that the Ibo and Yoruba are very different from one another. Answer 4 is the only option that lists two very different things.

LESSON 4, pp. 38–39

1. Comprehension: (2), In line 14, Mrs. Wright tells Mr. Hale that he cannot speak to John because John is dead.

2. Analysis: (4), A person would have a "word of comfort" for someone who is going through a difficult time. However, Goodman Parker does not have a word of comfort for Mary, who is also described as "a young woman in trouble," so he has no good news for her.

UNIT 2 (continued)

3. Comprehension: (1), The beginning of the excerpt describes Margaret as a widow, so we know that her husband is believed dead. At the end of the excerpt, Goodman Parker tells Margaret that her husband was among a number of men who were reportedly killed but are actually alive.

4. Synthesis: (5), Delaying the announcement makes the tension and suspension of the plot increase. Readers are likely sympathetic to Margaret's case, and want the news just as badly as she does.

5. Analysis: (3), You know Margaret has received the happy news that her husband is not dead. However, Mary is "a young woman in trouble," so it is likely she does not have good news. This plot element is likely to be a source of conflict between Margaret and Mary.

LESSON 5, pp. 40–41

1. Analysis: (5), Line 9 says that Mrs. Whipple "couldn't stand to be pitied." This indicates she is a proud woman who does not want other people to feel bad for her.

2. Comprehension: (4), Mrs. Slade is described as a woman who thought of herself as a "handsome woman with the good clothes." This indicates that she was proud of the social position that came with being the wife of a "famous corporation lawyer."

3. Synthesis: (1), Mrs. Slade does appear to be quite confident, but she also appears to be concerned only with material, superficial things, such as clothing. She also sounds very angry about the loss of her status in society.

4. Synthesis: (5), Readers can learn much about a character through his or her thoughts. The author probably intended for readers to get an idea about Mrs. Slade's personality by learning about her thoughts. The excerpt gives readers none of Mrs. Slade's actions or emotional reactions, so answers 3 and 4 are not correct. We also do not get other people's thoughts about Mrs. Slade, since the point of view is limited to Mrs. Slade's thoughts, so answers 1 and 2 are not correct.

5. Analysis: (3), Based on the context clues surrounding the phrase, you can assume that a "frump" is someone who does not take care of his or her appearance.

6. Application: (2), Mrs. Slade never mentions having a job, so answer 1 is incorrect. She also never says she ever had a job, so answer 3 is incorrect. Readers are never told if Mrs. Slade ever had children, so answer 4 is incorrect. Readers are also never told that Mrs. Slade volunteered to do anything, so answer 5 is incorrect.

LESSON 6, pp. 42–43

1. Analysis: (3), Based on line 12, in which we learn that Martha sees her mother "savoring…the vengeful triumph," we can assume that the mother does not want the children to get the family records and belongings.

2. Comprehension: (3), The last paragraph explains that Greenspahn is mad at Siggie for selling him bad cheese. He believes Siggie is doing this on purpose.

3. Synthesis: (2), Wholesalers would most likely throw away food that has gone bad, which would mean that they would take a loss on the product. However, if they sold a product that had gone bad, they would not lose that money.

4. Synthesis: (1), Siggie's sale of bad cheese to Greenspahn indicates that he is likely trying to avoid talking to Greenspahn about the products. There is no mention of Siggie's work habits, and he does not say that he is going to be late. Siggie and Shirley were talking before Greenspahn tried to get Siggie's attention. Siggie already gave Greenspahn a good deal if he was previously cheaper than the dairy (lines 33–35).

5. Analysis: (5), In line 15, Greenspahn tells Siggie, "I been getting complaints."

LESSON 7, pp. 44–45

1. Comprehension: (3), The author states that Connie "check[s] other people's faces to make sure her own was all right" and tells us that the mother "noticed everything and knew everything."

2. Comprehension: (4), The narrator explains that she is still in school, and that she lives with her parents.

3. Comprehension: (1), The pronoun "I" can only be used to tell the thoughts of one person. It also indicates first-person point of view.

4. Synthesis: (5), Readers do not learn anything about the rest of the family's feelings, so answer 1 is incorrect. There is no analysis of the father's bathing habits, so answer 2 is incorrect. There is no indication that the mother resents anything, so answer 3 is incorrect. Readers learn very little about how the girl feels about her parents; she simply observes their behaviors and describes them, so answer 4 is incorrect.

5. Application: (2), The narrator presents ordinary facts about her daily life, in much the same way that a person would write in his or her diary.

LESSON 8, pp. 46–47

1. Synthesis: (4), Lines 15 and 16 indicate the children know that the mother "could not feel love…not for anybody," as said in line 13. Her true feelings are not hidden from her children.

2. Analysis: (3), Donald is sparing people his bad moods and trying to cope with his memories of serving in the Vietnam War. He is haunted by his memories of what was done to the land and the people of Vietnam. These memories disrupt his life.

3. Comprehension: (2), Lines 4 through 7 state, "Vietnam had never seemed such a meaningful fact until a couple of years ago, when he grew depressed and moody."

UNIT 2 (continued)

4. Analysis: (1), Donald goes on to say that the war stripped off "the best part of the land and the country." This statement indicates he believes both the war and the strip mining are destructive actions.

5. Synthesis: (4), Donald's memories of Vietnam haunt him in the same way that a ghost might haunt a house.

6. Application: (5), At the end of the second paragraph, Donald is satisfied that coal companies have to plant trees and bushes to replace what they have taken from the land.

LESSON 9, *pp. 48–49*

1. Analysis: (4), The beginning of the excerpt describes the restaurant as a pretty place, and then explains its decorations.

2. Comprehension: (5), The end of the excerpt tells us that Hook can hear the Pacific Ocean from his location, so we know he must live near the ocean.

3. Application: (3), Hook's parents left to find a new place where they could get the resources they need to feed and take care of themselves. This is most like human parents moving to a new town to find a job.

4. Synthesis: (2), In this excerpt, the author is demonstrating how Hook is affected by his parents' abandonment of him. Describing Hook's environment in words that show the difficulty of finding food and fending for himself emphasizes the effect.

5. Synthesis: (4), Hook's parents make him change his location sooner than usual so that he can be closer to any food source that might be present. This is brought on by the lack of water and the potential lack of food that might result.

LESSON 10, *pp. 50–51*

1. Analysis: (4), The young man is described in funny, sympathetic terms. The author's tone is humorous.

2. Synthesis: (4), The author describes the scene in ominous and frightening terms. The tone is threatening.

3. Analysis: (2), The words "weird dawn" and "ungodly awakening" imply that something bad is likely to take place soon.

4. Application: (5), An omen is something which hints that something else will happen. A mystery tale is the most likely kind of story to have some sort of hint or foreshadowing of what is to come.

5. Comprehension: (1), Lines 28 and 29 state that the womens' songs "were cottonwads to stop their ears." People use cottonwads to muffle or avoid sounds, so the women were singing to drown out the affect of the dogs barking and roosters crowing in response to the full moon.

6. Analysis: (3), Earlier in the passage, the narrator says that Louisa was thinking about Bob and Tom, and that neither character alone had any "unusual significance." However, when she combined her thoughts of each man, she became agitated and restless.

LESSON 11, *pp. 52–53*

1. Comprehension: (4), Cows do not speak, but in this excerpt they are given dialogue, like humans. This is an example of personification.

2. Comprehension: (3), The character is comparing herself to a tree in the wind. The use of the phrase "as helpless as" indicates this is a simile.

3. Analysis: (2), The author is trying to describe how quickly the pain sets in—"running like a wildfire." The simile of the wildfire indicates its burning speed, as wildfires are prone to spread quickly.

4. Synthesis: (1), The author frequently uses figurative language to describe the feelings her character is experiencing, and she most frequently uses similes to do so.

5. Comprehension: (5), Lines 31 and 32 state, "the brain was as small as a seashell."

LESSON 12, *pp. 54–55*

1. Analysis: (2), The vulture eye has made the speaker so angry that he is willing to kill the old man to get rid of the eye.

2. Comprehension: (4), The noise of the plane is described as "roaring through the radio news," which implies that it was so loud the radio could not be heard.

3. Analysis: (1), The narrator describes the scene in exciting terms, as the characters rush out of the house to watch the plane, and says it was "the first close-up plane I ever saw" (lines 5–6). The plane symbolizes the excitement of something new.

4. Application: (4), Many people are intrigued by the sight of the plane and rush out to gawk. This is most like the arrival of a circus to town.

5. Synthesis: (3), The description of the fairgrounds explains why it is a good place for the plane to land. This image is best described as matter-of-fact.

LESSON 13, *pp. 56–57*

1. Analysis: (4), Marion interrupts Lincoln's attempts to gloss over the issues and instead directly asks Charlie about his drinking with an attitude.

2. Comprehension: (2), Nick gives Ole Anderson information about the people who have apparently come to kill Anderson. He wants to warn Anderson to keep him safe.

3. Analysis: (3), Ole Anderson is apparently accepting of the fact that these people are coming to kill him and does not react strongly.

4. Application: (1), Nick cares for Ole Anderson and does not want to see him killed by these men. He has come to share information with Anderson, much in the same way that someone might forward an e-mail that contains information concerning a friend.

5. Synthesis: (2), Ole Anderson's tone lets readers know he has accepted the idea that the men are here to kill him.

6. Analysis: (5), A person would offer to go to the police or describe the men as a form of help to a friend.

LESSON 14, *pp. 58–59*

1. Analysis: (1), Readers are told that Laird is cold, despite the heat of the day, and that his appearance has changed greatly. This indicates he is most likely suffering from a rare disease.

UNIT 2 (continued)

2. Analysis: (4), The doctor is speaking with Mrs. Wilson about her condition. Mrs. Wilson has tuned him out and is concentrating on her reaction to the news, which is why the doctor's voice sounds distant and muffled, as though through a can.

3. Synthesis: (5), The speaker's tone is lighthearted and sarcastic even after receiving bad news, which indicates that she has a sense of humor.

4. Comprehension: (3), The second paragraph provides hints about the speaker's condition. You know that both her breast and uterus are affected by her condition, that the doctors are going to have to "strip out the lymph nodes," and that she is likely to undergo chemotherapy. The speaker is most likely affected by cancer.

5. Application: (2), The speaker of the story receives bad news. This is most like a letter in the mail informing a character that he or she has failed a test.

LESSON 15, pp. 60–61
1. Analysis: (4), Most of the excerpt describes how Paul reacts to the music.

2. Comprehension: (4), The beginning of the excerpt explains that Mrs. Leslie and Belinda are used to country life, and then describes different aspects of country life. From this description and Leo's discomfort, you can assume that Leo is in the country.

3. Synthesis: (2), The phrase "yet another" picnic lets us know that Leo has attended more than one of the picnics, and indicates his impatience with them. Leo will most likely dislike the next picnic to which he is invited.

4. Application: (3), Leo is out of his element and does not know entirely what to do, as he has no prior experience in this sort of situation. He is most like a big city lawyer on a trail ride who does not know how to saddle his horse.

5. Analysis: (5), You may know that some people take pride in having artifacts that have been passed down through their families for generations. Mrs. Leslie's constant references to the age of the picnic basket indicate that she likes to brag about her family.

UNIT 2 REVIEW, pp. 62–65
1. Synthesis: (3), The last sentence of the excerpt states that the speaker is "stuck in Vera Cruz." While he has accepted his fate, he is quite annoyed with it, which makes "stranded" the best answer option.

2. Comprehension: (4), Lines 1 through 4 of the excerpt let us know that the speaker has been busy for a while and that the idea of having nothing to do is amusing.

3. Analysis: (3), A slate is like a chalkboard that can be erased, and a sponge is often used to wash down and erase a slate or a chalkboard. Based on this information, you can assume that the speaker wants his mind to be erased.

4. Synthesis: (1), The speaker wishes to not be stuck in Vera Cruz and that he were able to forget things. He also wishes he could choose his moment of laziness and have his surroundings exactly as he would want them. However, he has apparently accepted the fact that he is stuck for the time being and does not seem to be annoyed. His tone is best described as wishful.

5. Analysis: (2), The pearl is described as being "priceless," but rather than ingest it herself, Cleopatra gave the drink with the pearl to Antony. This action shows she cared for him more than for herself.

6. Application: (5), The speaker has a wish: to continue his trip and leave Vera Cruz; but his wish is not fulfilled because of the dock strike. His situation is most like that of a customer who wants to buy an item that is not available to her.

7. Analysis: (4), The sisters' lives are being compared. Bessie's life is determined to be richer, even though she did not have as much as Lottie did, while Lottie is described as lacking, even though she always had money.

8. Analysis: (5), Lines 51 and 52 state that Lottie believed a "job in hand was worth two in the future," indicating that she would prefer financial security to job happiness.

9. Synthesis: (2), The author is describing the differences between each woman's approach to wealth.

10. Comprehension: (5), Lottie is described as always having been secure in her wealth.

11. Application: (4), Bess is described as a woman who took what life had to offer immediately, since she was content to stay with a man who had little ambition and married him right out of high school, when she might have waited a few years and married a man who could have made more money or made her happier. Her situation is most like someone who fills up on appetizers instead of waiting for the meal.

12. Analysis: (2), Lottie is described as never being wasteful. Even as a child, she denied herself simple pleasures such as ice cream because she considered them unnecessary and preferred to save her money.

UNIT 3 POETRY

LESSON 1, pp. 68–69
1. Analysis: (3), If you read the poem out loud, you should notice that your speech patterns fall into a steady, regular pattern of stressed and unstressed syllables.

2. Analysis: (1), The poet was most likely attempting to make readers laugh at the sudden and unexpected rhyme.

3. Synthesis: (3), Lines 1 through 3 each contain eight syllables, and line 5 has nine syllables. These lines of similar lengths create a predictable rhythm that is thrown off slightly by line 4, and is completely thrown off by the abrupt ending.

4. Comprehension: (3), The poet chose a formal rhythm that matches her very proper language to contrast with the ending of the poem, in which she asks for one perfect limousine.

UNIT 3 (continued)

5. Application: (4), The poem suggests that the speaker would prefer a more useful or material object, such as a limousine. The poem also indicates that the speaker has particular tastes, so she would probably most like a jewelry store gift certificate.

LESSON 2, pp. 70–71

1. Analysis: (4), The poet states that books "take us lands away" (line 2). The comparison means that a book can take its readers on adventures, much like a ship can take passengers on adventures.

2. Comprehension: (3), Lines 15 through 20 explain that the speaker and his friend are thinking of the people they both knew who are no longer living.

3. Analysis: (5), Typically, it is easier to pick or gather fruit that hangs toward the bottom of the tree, so the fruit at the top of the tree is usually there the longest. In this poem, the two or three berries refer to the few members of the speaker's circle of friends who are still alive.

4. Synthesis: (3), *Wistful* means "wishing or longing for something." In the poem, the speaker is wishing that more of his friends were still alive. The poet is not angry or disappointed, so answers 1 and 2 are incorrect. The speaker does not indicate that he is afraid of anything, so answer 4 is incorrect. The poem does end with merry jests, but there is a hint of sadness present, so the speaker is not joyous; therefore, answer 5 is incorrect.

5. Application: (1), The meeting is some sort of celebration, but the people there are constantly remembering the people who are no longer with them. This is most like a person trying, but failing, to enjoy her own birthday party.

LESSON 3, pp. 72–73

1. Analysis: (2), Cats are known for being quiet, so the poet uses the image of the fog walking like a cat to emphasize its quiet appearance.

2. Synthesis: (3), Fog cannot sit, and it has no haunches, but describing the fog in this manner gives readers an idea of how it appears to the poet and helps them to identify with the feeling and tone of the poem.

3. Comprehension: (1), Lines 13 through 16 tell us that the speaker would spend hundreds and even thousands of years devoted to his mistress.

4. Synthesis: (3), No person could live for the amount of time that is described in the passage, yet the speaker insists that he would love this woman for ages.

5. Application: (5), The speaker uses hyperbole to emphasize the depth of his love for his mistress. Love cannot physically grow, so it cannot be vaster than an empire, in much the same way that a person cannot give the moon to another person.

6. Analysis: (3), The speaker knows that for all the time he would spend with his mistress, he cannot escape time, and it will continue to pass.

LESSON 4, pp. 74–75

1. Analysis: (1), The image of the battered knuckle gives readers the idea that the father has probably recently punched someone or something, like a wall.

2. Comprehension: (1), In line 3, the traveler asks about the day's journey.

3. Analysis: (3), An easy trip would not leave people feeling travel-sore and weak, so answer 1 is incorrect. The poem states that the journey is uphill all the way to the end, so answer 2 is incorrect. There is also no indication that the traveler is on horseback or in a car, so answers 4 and 5 are incorrect as well.

4. Analysis: (4), In poetry, a road is often a symbol of life's journey. The first stanza gives a hint—the road only goes one way, uphill, and it will take an entire day, or one lifespan.

5. Application: (2), The second speaker indicates that travelers are always welcome at this inn, in much the same way that someone might say "the door is always open."

6. Synthesis: (5), The first speaker asks if he must knock or call when he approaches the door, and the second speaker lets him know that he will not even have to wait. This is a comforting thought to someone who has traveled a long time.

LESSON 5, pp. 76–77

1. Analysis: (2), From the last stanza, you can infer that the speaker's love has likely died.

2. Comprehension: (3), The speaker says, "between my knees my forehead was." If you rearrange this phrase to read "my forehead was between my knees," you will understand that he is sitting with his head between his knees.

3. Analysis: (1), Line 13 indicates that the speaker is experiencing "perfect grief."

4. Analysis: (2), The speaker is on a hilltop staring at some weeds (lines 9 and 10). He is so blinded by his unconsoled grief (lines 13 and 14) that the only thing that holds his attention is the woodspurge.

5. Synthesis: (4), You might know that the word *desolate* means "extremely empty or sad," which would describe the poem's tone. If you did not know the meaning of desolate, you can make inferences to rule out the other answer options. The tone is not confused, nor forgiving. A feeling of grief is an extreme feeling, while indifference is a lack of interest. The speaker does not want to fight anyone, so the tone is not combative.

6. Comprehension: (5), Lines 3 and 4 state that the speaker walked at the wind's will. He was paying no attention to where he was walking, simply moving as the wind pushed him.

LESSON 6, pp. 78–79

1. Comprehension: (1), The second stanza describes what happens "if you tuck the name of a loved one / under your tongue," or keep that person in your thoughts. Lines 15 and 16 imply that the fuel or energy a person "feeds" on comes from a person he or she loves.

2. Comprehension: (3), Line 1 tells us the speaker is standing on a tower. You can infer that the speaker is implying the time is New Year's Eve, when an old year and a new year "meet."

UNIT 3 (continued)

3. Analysis: (2), From this line, you can assume that the speaker has had a difficult year and is in tears as the years change over.

4. Comprehension: (3), In lines 6 and 7, the speaker states that there's been enough science and exploration. "Aught" is an old term for "anything." From this information, you can restate the stanza as "Have we learned anything that is useful and worth knowing?"

5. Application: (4), The speaker is concerned about the amount of information that has become available, and questions whether it is worth knowing. This is similar to the way that a parent might try to cope with rapidly changing technology.

6. Synthesis: (2), The speaker of the poem questions whether things are worth knowing, and the descriptions in the poem are uncomfortable, with the storm and the wind roaring. The tone of the poem is best identified as "uneasy."

LESSON 7, pp. 80–81

1. Synthesis: (5), The theme of the poem can be inferred from the first line: "Your world is as big as you make it." The speaker means that people can limit themselves to a small area or small ideas, or they can dream big.

2. Analysis: (2), The speaker says, "[m]ere anarchy is loosed upon the world" in line 4. The speaker believes that events in the world are creating an unstable environment, in which the center is falling apart and cannot hold together.

3. Comprehension: (3), The tone of the poem indicates that the speaker is worried about how events of the time will lead to the destruction of world.

4. Synthesis: (1), These lines can be restated as "The people who have the best intentions lack the conviction to speak up, while the people who have the worst intentions are shouting at the tops of their lungs." The speaker is most likely implying that people with the worst intentions are those who speak the loudest, so answer 1 is the best, most complete option.

5. Synthesis: (4), The first stanza explains how everything is falling apart and the speaker feels that mankind is to blame: "anarchy is loosed upon the world," "the ceremony of innocence is drowned," and "the worst / Are full of passionate intensity." The second stanza discusses the Second Coming, which is a reference to an apocalypse that will end the world. The theme of this poem is best stated as "The evil of men will bring about the end of the world."

UNIT 3 REVIEW, pp. 82–85

1. Comprehension: (2), The speaker implies that he has been gone for five years and has missed the sound of the water trickling through the river bed.

2. Synthesis: (3), The speaker indicates that he is alone at the site, saying that his thoughts lean towards more seclusion (lines 5–7) and comparing himself to a hermit (lines 21–22).

3. Analysis: (5), These lines can be restated as "I'm sitting here, under this sycamore tree, again." This tells readers that the speaker came to this location previously.

4. Synthesis: (1), The speaker tells readers that he has been to this place before, and describes all the things he remembers about the place and their current appearance.

5. Analysis: (4), The speaker does not tell readers about any religious ideas he may follow, so answer 1 is incorrect. The speaker also gives no indication that his family is dead, so answer 2 is incorrect. The speaker describes the setting as a place he has been before and likely knows his way around, so answer 3 is incorrect. Nothing in the poem indicates that the speaker is writing about history, so answer 5 is incorrect.

6. Application: (3), The speaker shows a great appreciation for the natural beauty of the countryside around him, and indicates that he has been to this location before. He would most likely enjoy a visit to the country while on a holiday.

7. Comprehension: (1), The speaker says, "Natural and things / and spiritual, —who separates those two…[t]ears up the bond of nature and brings death." This indicates that the speaker believes that the natural and the spiritual should not be divided.

8. Synthesis: (3), The poet uses symbolism and imagery to show how life must be balanced between the natural and the spiritual. For instance, the image of the apple, which in this poem represents life ("This apple of life," line 10), is destroyed when it is cut in half and divided: "The perfect round which fitted Venus' hand / Has perished as utterly as if we ate / both halves" (lines 11–13).

9. Analysis: (4), In line 10, the author says, "This apple of life."

10. Synthesis: (2), The poet firmly argues her case for the union of the natural and the spiritual parts of life, but does so through the use of examples of beauty and art. This indicates that she is most likely determined to get her point across to her readers.

11. Analysis: (5), From the context of the poem and the information provided in the question, you can assume that Antinous was a beautiful Greek man who was born into the lower classes of society. The poet's reference to Antinous indicates that she believes something beautiful can come from an ordinary background.

12. Application: (1), The poet believes that beautiful art can and should come from natural objects that have a sort of spirituality. Given her examples of marble and clay statues, the author would most likely choose to take up wood carving as a hobby.

UNIT 4 DRAMA

LESSON 1, pp. 88–89

1. Comprehension: (4), The location of the play is part of the background information of the exposition.

2. Analysis: (3), The child first says "Today is the day of atonement." A few lines later, Faustus wishes that he and his family could be returned to earth, whole and restored. This indicates that the family has died, and this conversation is most likely taking place before the gates of Heaven.

3. Analysis: (2), Faustus's petition and plea is that his family be returned to earth, whole and restored.

UNIT 4 (continued)

4. Synthesis: (2), Faustus obviously loves his family, and he is pleading with the angel to allow his family to return to earth.

LESSON 2, pp. 90–91

1. Comprehension: (2), Muffett tells the other characters about Rita's weight, which had no part in the conversation before. Muffett is a gossip.

2. Analysis: (4), The taximan asks Liza if she can read, which indicates that the fare is plainly stated. Liza most likely cannot read.

3. Comprehension: (2), Liza has trouble accepting the taxi fare for a short ride, which indicates that it is more than she wants to spend. The description of her apartment also indicates that she has financial difficulties. Liza is best described as impoverished.

4. Synthesis: (4), Liza likely makes a limited wage, and knows that she has to have four shillings every week for rent. She must have to carefully account for all her money.

LESSON 3, pp. 92–93

1. Comprehension: (3), Wining Boy's motivation is most likely to sell the suit and make some money quickly.

2. Analysis: (4), Lines 20 through 24 indicate that Cyrano believes there is something wrong with him that would make him undeserving of even the plainest woman's love.

3. Comprehension: (3), Lines 9 through 11 tell you Cyrano has hated Silenus since he looked at Cyrano's love.

4. Application: (1), Cyrano describes the woman in complimentary words, in much the same way that an art critic would describe a masterful piece of art.

5. Synthesis: (2), In lines 20 through 24, Cyrano explains that he believes the woman could not possibly love him because of his nose. He most likely helps Christian because he feels that the woman could never love him.

LESSON 4, pp. 94–95

1. Synthesis: (2), The main argument between Meridian and Lorenzo is whether Parnell can be trusted because he is white. The theme of the excerpt is best stated in answer 2.

2. Comprehension: (5), Mr. Frank most likely knows that Anne could get caught if she is seen moving about the downstairs.

3. Synthesis: (1), You know that the family is staying upstairs and not going downstairs because of the fear of being caught. Yet Anne finds great joy in the gift her father has given her. Answer 1 best states the theme of the excerpt.

4. Application: (4), From the excerpt, you can assume that Anne loves to write, but that she had not had anything in which to write before her father gave her the diary. Her situation is most like that of a poor musician receiving a new guitar.

LESSON 5, pp. 96–97

1. Comprehension: (3), Hugh is aggravated that Annabelle will not give him the attention he wants and answers his question in a roundabout way, but he is not really angry with her. His tone is best described as aggravated.

2. Analysis: (3), Jack defends Miss Cardew when Algernon speaks of her in an offensive way. His tone is protective.

3. Analysis: (2), Algernon is quite sarcastic and almost bitter as he talks to Jack about Miss Cardew and Jack's clothes.

4. Synthesis: (1), Based on the poet's choice of words, you can assume that the men are good friends who are used to one another's attitudes. The feeling of the excerpt is best described as friendly.

LESSON 6, pp. 98–99

1. Comprehension: (1), The citizens of the town are angry and violent, and Capulet and Montague are very angry with one another.

2. Comprehension: (3), Margaret and Brick are tense and aggravated, and described as though they have been "broken apart from a violent struggle."

3. Analysis: (4), Brick lashes out at Margaret, demanding his crutch. His actions indicate that he is bad-tempered, likely because he needs a crutch to walk.

4. Analysis: (1), Based on Margaret's speech, it seems as though Brick has been behaving coolly towards her, and so she regards his moment of excitement as a good sign that he is warming up to her.

UNIT 4 REVIEW, pp. 100–103

1. Comprehension: (2), Oscar is irritated with the other characters' actions.

2. Synthesis: (3), At the end of the excerpt, Oscar says that the old gang is changing and breaking up. The group is not having its ritual poker game as frequently as they used to.

3. Application: (4), Felix is very clean, even disinfecting the playing cards. If Felix were to go on a date, he would likely go to a very clean restaurant that had received good reviews.

4. Comprehension: (1), Lines 34 through 42 indicate that Roy is bothered by the smell of disinfectant.

5. Analysis: (3), Felix is not messy, so answer 1 is incorrect. He is not described as being overly emotional and happy, so answer 2 is incorrect. Felix is not described as being disgusted, so answer 4 is incorrect. In the excerpt, Felix does not have many lines, which is partly because he is in another room, but he may not be a quiet character, so answer 5 is not the best option.

6. Analysis: (5), Vinnie states "No, I guess no one feels like playing much lately" (lines 47–48), and Murray puts on his shoes to get ready to go (lines 52–53). Based on this exchange and the way Roy left, you can assume that Vinnie and Murray both left.

7. Comprehension: (4), Golde chastises Chava for reading, saying that it will not get her a better husband, and she is hopeful that Yente has found a good match for Tzeitel. Golde is intent on making sure her daughters get married.

8. Analysis: (3), Golde obviously did not want Shprintze to put the basket on her head, so her tone is sarcastic.

9. Analysis: (3), Yente is very excited about her news, describing it as "not just every-day-in-the-week news—once-in-a-lifetime news."

10. Analysis: (4), From Golde's dialogue after she spits between her fingers, you can assume her action is similar to knocking on wood to ward off bad luck.

11. Synthesis: (2), Yente is very active in her attempts to make matches between the young men and women of the town. Based on the excerpt, she could be best described as an active busy-body.

12. Application: (5), Chava enjoys reading a great deal, so much so that she hides her books from her mother. She would most likely enjoy a career as a librarian.

13. Synthesis: (1), Golde is intent on finding good matches for all her children, and would most likely complain that Chava is not interested enough in this pursuit.

14. Comprehension: (4), Tzeitel points out that she is not even twenty years old, and that the men Yente usually finds are not what she wants in a husband. She is most concerned with being married at what she considers to be a young age.

Index

Note: Page numbers in **boldface** indicate definitions or main discussion. Page ranges indicate examples and practice.

INDEX

INDEX

Point of view
of fiction, **44**, 44–45
of nonfiction, **20**, 20–21
Predictions, 60, 98
Prior knowledge, 16, 76
Progression, 8
Protagonist, **90**
Punctuation
inserting to restate, 78
rhythm created through, 68
Purpose, 20, 24

R

Reading skills
apply ideas, **60**, 60–61
categorizing, **6**, 6–7
cause/effect, **10**, 10–11, **34**, 34–35
compare/contrast, **12**, 12–13, **36**, 36–37
determine point of view, **20**, 20–21, **44**, 44–45
distinguish fact from opinion, **14**, 14–15
draw conclusions, **18**, 18–19, **58**, 58–59
generalize, **24**, 24–25
identify plot elements, **38**, 38–39
main idea/details, **2**, 2–3
make inferences, **16**, 16–17, **56**, 56–57, **76**, 76–77
restatement, **78**, 78–79
sequencing, **8**, 8–9
style/tone, **22**, 22–23
summarize, **4**, 4–5
understanding plot, **88**, 88–89
using context clues, **32**, 32–33
Repetition, 22
Resolution, **38**, **88**
Restatement
determining words' meanings from, 32
of poetry, **78**, 78–79
summarizing, 4
Rhyme, **68**, 68–69
Rhyming patterns, 68
Rhythm, **68**, 68–69

S

Scenery, 87
Scientific writing, 14
Sensory words. *See* Imagery
Sequence, **8**, 8–9
Setting
effect on tone, 50
information about in exposition, 88
of fiction, **48**, 48–49
Signal words
for cause/effect, 10, 34
for facts/opinions, 14
for generalizations, 24
for sequences, 8
for similarities/differences, 12
for similes, 52, 70

See also Key words
Similes, **52**, **70**
Song lyrics, 67
Sound effects
onomatopoeia, 52
rhythm and rhyme, 68
Stage directions
in plays, **90**
mood revealed through, 98
tone revealed through, 96
understanding characters' actions through, 87
Stanzas, 67, **68**
Statistics, 2
Style, **22**, 22–23
Summarize, **4**, 4–5
Supporting details. *See* Details
Symbols
in fiction, **54**, 54–55
in poetry, 72, **74**, 74–75
making inferences and, 76, 80
Synonyms, 32

T

Test-taking tips
analyzing point of view, 44
answer all questions, x
author's purpose, 20
categorizing setting details, 48
clues to characters' personalities, 40
clues to conflicts, 56
complications, 38
correctly complete answer sheet, x
determining sequences, 8
drawing conclusions, 58
identifying imagery, 74
identifying motivations, 42
identifying themes, 80
interpreting tone, 96
organizing comparisons/contrasts, 36
reading for personification, 72
reading poetry aloud, 68
understanding characters in plays, 90
use of figurative language, 52
using synonyms, 32
Theme
of drama, **94**, 94–95
of fiction, **46**, 46–47
of poetry, **80**, 80–81
Things as symbols, 54
Timeline, 8
Time of story, 48
Tone
determining validity of generalizations, 24
mood and, 98
of drama, **96**, 96–97
of fiction, **50**, 50–51
of nonfiction, **22**, 22–23
Topic sentence, 2

U

Unit reviews, 26–29, 62–65, 82–85, 100–103
analyzing analogies, 70
categorizing, 6
connecting keywords/details, 10
determining cause/effect, 34
determining character motivation, 92
determining climax/resolution, 88
determining main idea of play, 94
determining tone of nonfiction, 22
finding main idea/details, 2
making inferences, 16, 76
predicting characters' actions, 60
reading for tone, 50
understanding symbols, 54
use clues from mood to predict, 98

V

Venn diagrams, 12, 36
Vocabulary. *See* Language

W

Word choices. *See* Figurative language; Key words; Language; Signal words